CW00925157

Grief to Grit

A touching tale of love, loss, pain & tenacity

Claris N. Angafor

Grief to Grit

Authored by Claris N. Angafor
©copyright Claris N.Angafor 2020

Edited by Marcia M Publishing House Editorial Team Published by
Marcia M Spence of Marcia M Publishing House, West Bromwich, West
Midlands the UNITED KINGDOM B71

All rights reserved 2020 Marcia M Publishing House

First published November 2020

*Claris N. Angafor asserts the moral right to be identified as the author of
this work. The opinions expressed in this published work are those of
the author and do not reflect the opinions of Marcia M Publishing
House or its editorial team.*

*This book is sold subject to the conditions it is not, by way of trade or
otherwise, lent, hired out or otherwise circulated in any form of binding
or cover other than that in which it is published. No part of this
publication may be reproduced, stored in a retrieval system or
transmitted in any form or by any means (electronic, mechanical,
photocopying, recording or otherwise) without prior written permission
from the Author or Publisher.*

MARCIA M
PUBLISHING HOUSE

www.marciampublishing.com

Dedication

To Davi-Jayce Ancheitiimbom Angafor whose life and death gave a clearer meaning to the purpose of my experiences and my journey of self-discovery. It had to take his death for me to be reborn;

Without your existence, there would have been no grief to GRIT;

To Angel Angafor whom I never met but whose memories will live forever.

To all Angel Babies; known and Unknown.

To Lesra and Gicles, my greatest challengers and loveliest companions;

To my beloved husband Giddeon; who has been a source of support all through our journeys.

Without you all, this book would have been incomplete.

Lastly, my parents: Bobe Michael Mbeng, Nawain Bibiana Natang, Mr. Samdim George and Mrs. S. Mbeng Matilda

And all who played a role in my upbringing and education.

Acknowledgements

Thanking God Almighty for giving me the road map each time I needed one.

My Gratitude goes first of all to Marcia Publishing House and her team for working so hard and for selecting my manuscript for publication.

This manuscript would have remained at this stage without the input of this interesting and talented young man, Nkwain Killian Tubuo. His time, dedication and above all respect for my being and my opinion played a huge role in us working together.

There are many who supported me both financially, spiritually and emotionally all through my journey right up to the point of writing this book.

Fr. Innocent Akum Wefon went through the original manuscript which was so raw with emotions. He encouraged and pushed me to turn it into a book.

Sister Imma Anguo and the rest of the family in Luton, you all know how much you mean to me and words can never describe it

Appreciations go to Lin Rogers; my former manager for all the support she gave me while I worked at RBH and when I was unwell.

I appreciate Christabel for bringing baby Jayden Home during the week leading to Davi-Jayce turning 3 in Heaven. This played a huge role in our grief journey. I felt so much relief looking after our grandson.

The medical team at Basingstoke Hospital (Delivery/Bereavement Suite): Dr. Ian Simpson, Jess Rogers, Jess Lorrain, Catherine McIntyre, Layla Fraser, Rachel Stoodley, Nagih Rostrun, Miss Sohail, Dr.Ilori Oladotun, Dr. Priya, Fiona Jackson, Daisy Weckworth,

Caroline Loxton, Sophie Waite. You all make an amazing team. As a family, we will always be grateful to you all for the care, love, support and compassion shown to us during and after my stay at the hospital.

When I reached out to some of my friends who have lost a baby in the past, they didn't hesitate to share their stories.

Sister Imma Anguo (UK), Grace Chebe (UK), Marie A. Abanga (Cameroon), Judith Moor (UK) and Nellyma Agathoz (Kenya). Thank you so much for sharing your journeys with me.

I sincerely thank and appreciate everyone who has played a part in this journey especially those who visited me in Hospital, those who held my hand, offered me a shoulder to cry on and those who lovingly wiped and kissed my tears away and even shed some with me when it became unbearable. And more especially to those who took care of my family while I was in hospital. I love and appreciate you all. In this light, I will very much like to thank Vincent Besong for his unending love, and moral support.

I cannot conclude this without acknowledging my Makeup artist; Patience Abonge and My photographer; Hippolitus Zama. You two did an amazing job for my cover photos.

Thanking God Almighty for giving me the road map each time I needed one for all the journeys I have travelled.

May God abundantly bless you all.

Table of Contents

Preface

Grief to Grit is an informative read, conveying a mother's account of the loss of her fourth child. It takes you into the deep world and roller coaster of emotions that she felt. The emotions are really well expressed, very raw and shared in a heartfelt manner. Claris' sadness can be felt alongside other emotions of anger, frustration, and eventual acceptance. She expresses the grit and determination needed, to highlight that the topic of baby loss should be talked about more openly and in a kind and understanding manner. Also, women should not feel silenced when grieving the loss of a child at any stage of pregnancy or post-birth.

It is a touching tale of love, loss and pain, expectations and disappointments. It tells of the joy that love brings to all but also carefully points out the pain that loss can bring into a family and the shadow of sadness that engulfs everyone in the household in these circumstances.

When Claris lost DJ, the pain threatened the joy of the love that she has for all around her. She had to go back in time to trace where all the love began. In losing her baby, she almost lost herself, and she lost faith in God, friends and family. Her self-confidence was completely diminished.

Towards the end of the memoir, she tells us how she conquered grief and gained grit. I am sure this book will be used as a reference source by those who grieve in one way or another

Claris says: "It's my hope that sharing my grief journey will raise awareness, help other grieving parents and help people learn how to morally support their loved ones who are going through grief or some other form of hardship or tough times."

Chapter One
Roots: Where it all Started

Giddeon, my movie man, is out of this place called earth. When he talks, I want to put him on replay: his voice dripping of honey and words rolling out in slow-mo like he's got the universe under a spell. Yeah, I said that, under a spell. After all these years of sipping his breath every morning, watching him smile like a baby, seeing him go mute in anger, having his muscles shield me, frowning at his imperfections, glowing with pride at his pluses, going through thick and thin together, and all that, Giddeon still has me under this spell. Even when he drives me crazy, I find myself asking for a seatbelt because, with him, it always ends up as a great ride. You now see what a spell can do, don't you? Like, I literally still have a crush on this man, and I don't plan ever recovering from that. He's ebony black with a dazzling smile I can't resist. Gentle Giddeon is still the man in my pillow when the world wears me out and turns me off. He's like wine in every sense of it. Not just any type of wine, though. I just pray you never get to ask me what my favourite wine is. When I talk to God, I ask him to keep my glass full. I want to be sipping through the shine and pour. So, the sipping, you must know by now, is what I keep constant as we grey.

Yeah, I can see your eyes rolling out that 'how-did-you-meet' cliché thing. Well, Giddeon and I, we've come a long way. We've been through so much. Undying love has been our bond. Throw stones at us, and we'll give you milestones.' That's been the unsaid, yet mutually understood code of us. Back to your question, well I can tell you he was in a seminary undergoing training to become a priest when we met?

Mill Hill was where he was studying theology. The first time I set eyes on this sweet and adorable criminal (yes, he stole my heart and I'm stuck with him) was in church. Hey, don't be surprised. Haven't you been told love happens in strange places?

Giddeon and his friends had a particular pew on which they sat in church every Sunday. I was quick to notice this consistency and found it amazing and intriguing. To me, Giddeon was the G in their glow. Slow down, go back and take him off and see how pathetic they would look. Ouch! Believe me, it's not like I'm wicked. But, you know what love does to people, don't you?

Whenever I walked into the church, my eyes knew exactly where to search as my heart raced. Seeing the crew with Gi present, always left my face wreathed in smiles that I had no control over as I quietly walked to my seat. Oh, this stupid thing called love! And, yes, that was how I started my services. It wasn't like I thought we could ever be together. Far from that, I just... Oh my God, what am I even saying? The truth is I still don't know what I was thinking or doing. All I know is my heart was somewhere and I had to let it pull my flesh along.

Then, the Lord smiled at me when Gi's leg got fractured. I'd be lying if I told you something else. Behold, after mass one Sunday morning, I saw him limping. This, I told myself, was my shot at talking to him for two reasons: on the one hand, I felt bad for him; on the other, a part of me couldn't resist the urge to sidle up to him and sympathise so he could know I existed. I mustered the courage.

'Good morning, brother?' I said blushing.

He turned around quickly with a face that bore no trace of surprise. He looked more handsome at a close range than I'd thought. I was nervous.

'Good morning. How are you?' he asked.

'I'm fine. What happened to your leg?' I managed.

'Actually, we were playing football and I fractured it.'

'I'm sorry.'

All my muses were failing me, so I decided to leave immediately before saying something embarrassing.

'Wait,' he took me by surprise. 'What is your name?'

'Claris.'

He went on to ask where I lived, and I told him. He told me his name, too. That was how we met.

Guiddeon, is how I would spell his name based on how it sounded to me. From that day, it became customary for us to say hello to each other every Sunday after mass before separating. I would later get to find out he was a second-year student at the Mill Hill Missionaries.

So, it goes without saying that what we had was purely platonic. He was a friend I really liked and would think about for long hours during my quiet moments, letting a thin smile flicker across my face. Brief Sunday-after-mass conversations became too shallow and my friend started paying us visits at home on Saturday and Sunday evenings.

Where I was raised, most parents considered it improper for a boy to visit a girl in their house; however, it was different for me. I was naïve, innocent and straightforward, which made it easy for me to be trusted at home. The few courageous and sincere male friends I had could always visit me at home without any fear. So, as you already know, Gi was one, and a brother for that matter.

You don't expect me to start explaining to you how sweet it felt having a brother call every weekend. Oh, those days! Did I mention to you he was fond of moving with this small umbrella? We found it a bit funny and nicknamed him The-Brother-With-The-Small-Umbrella.

The-Brother-With-The-Small-Umbrella once came and found me sleeping and recuperating on the sofa, all helpless. My high flat top haircut, which was trendy at the time, was a bit out of shape. The picture of me in my short old *kaba (dressing gown-like)* stretched on the sofa still makes me smirk like Cinderella every time it sneaks up on me. Well, I guess we all have such moments only death can delete from our hard drives. That funny after-intravenous-infusion-feeling still had me broken when my eyes awoke to find another pair unblinkingly staring into my face. The look in his eyes was quite intense. I couldn't believe he was by my side. The timing was just perfect. I still don't know, but there was something about his presence that made me just want to get up and start running about despite my frailty. I don't know if I should say therapeutic, but there was that healing effect somewhere deep in me. All I could do was let a weak smile tug at the corner of my mouth. Maybe I thought that was the coolest thing to do at that time. Please, don't ask me; I'm just as confused as to why it was like that.

The-Brother-With-The-Small-Umbrella ended up introducing me to all his friends as time went by. Don't give me that look, as a 'female friend,' of course. That was it. No bias, of course, but believe me when I say he was the most handsome of all the seminarians. I remember one of the priests at Mill Hill, whom I came to know as Fr Tom. His rector would call me Giddeon's Eve, whatever that meant. Whenever I think of it, I heave a sigh of relief that we don't grow apples in Bambui. Perhaps, an Eve with a mango wouldn't be such a repulsive sight. The following years brought surprises that my wildest imagination couldn't have guessed.

Mobile phones were not easy to come by back in those days, so my elder sister (Matilda) sent me to Bafut, a neighbouring tribe, to deliver a message to a family friend who was a priest. Guess who stood at the door welcoming me inside? No way, the shock churned in me as I tried hard to ward it off and act cool. My acting was pretty pathetic. Within my seemingly composed chest, my heart was dwarfing Usain Bolt. Giddeon was visibly surprised.

'What brings you here?' he asked.

'My elder sister sent me with a message for the priest,' I managed.

'He's not around,' he told me.

He was having his lunch when I arrived, so he invited me in to join him. After lunch, we sat in the priest's house and chatted for some time. Did I say chat, a question and answer session would be more apt. Given how shy I was, I waited for him to speak or ask a question before I could reply. After every reply, I would withdraw into my listener shell and just smile with my head down. It got a bit sensitive and deep at one point.

'Do you have a boyfriend?'

'No.'

'Have you ever been touched by a boy before?' I understood what he meant.

'No.'

It was getting a bit late and I had some distance to cover, though not on foot. Something somewhere in me wanted to stay by his side. I might have been shy, but I just felt complete sitting there with him. Some fibre deep in me was scared of messing things up and leaving him bored, though. I had to leave, in any case.

So, I summoned the courage and he rose to see me off without protesting. Gentle and meek, that was him. As we were walking out of the room, he quietly seized my hand unannounced and gently pressed his lips against mine.

Breath of life over bread of life? My electrocuted soul relished something I couldn't place a finger on. It was something far bigger than I. My upbringing and education screamed that I shove him away and never forgive him. The Claris I knew would have fought him with all the energy left in her. There I stood, however dreaming, yearning for more, holding my breath, savouring it all. If only I had the soul to tear myself away, the shy and guilty me would later think in a quiet corner.

I felt the essence of my whole being summarised in a few seconds. How on earth could I resist this man? I mean, how do you expect the honeybee to resist nectar? I hated him for leaving me that helpless; I hated him because I loved him that much; I hated him for sneaking up in my dreams uninvited; I hated him for looking that cute. I just so hated him for kidnapping the good kid in me. I hated him so much I didn't have to shut my eyes to see his face smiling back at me, making me smile as well. Perhaps, that was just the little silly girl in me making too big a deal out of what apparently appeared to be the accident of an unguarded moment. Excuse my French, but shit happens. It was an almost impossible decision, but I resolved not to expect anything from him. Our paths were different, and we had to stick to that.

Fast-forward to my university days (22-year-old, studying Management at the University of Buea, Cameroon). I don't mean to brag, but as a young girl, my presence almost always commanded that second look from the opposite sex (Well, even at 43 now, it still does). I might have been innocent, but I wasn't dumb. You get the difference, didn't you? Growing up–young, beautiful and broke–was sweet and painful. I wasn't really excited about the world of men and going to parties.

To start with, my meagre pocket allowance, when I had some, wasn't enough for me to afford the luxury of purchasing good party clothes or shoes, let alone money for snacks. Remember I said I was as pretty as a picture. That meant I could get almost anything I wanted from most of my male admirers. That did not sit well with me, though, for the simple reason that I had been brought up to understand that there's no free lunch. That stuck and no amount of peer pressure ever came anywhere close to uprooting it. I wasn't quite moved by so many things. If I had to get into any relationship, I needed the terms to be very clear.

All this greatly curbed the rate at which I went out to socialise. As for Gi, our relationship continued as platonic until he left for Uganda to pursue his studies. We both preferred it that way. Besides, I had made a vow to myself never to date a priest or a seminarian. We remained in touch; but it was not as before. We seldom wrote to each other. The few times we communicated; the letters came from him.

Life was so-so and my studies were great. My sister (Angeline) decided to pay me a visit from Douala. I picked her up after school and we headed for my hostel. As I opened the door, I saw a handwritten note unusually lying on the floor. The moment I picked it up and took a closer look at it, my heart pounded against my ribcage. I could tell exactly who the author was. Giddeon, how come? He was supposed to be in Uganda, not Cameroon. Given that I had heard from him a good number of times, I could tell it was his handwriting under the faint light of the moon. Could this be someone pulling a stunt on me?

'This cannot be true,' I muttered to myself.

'What cannot be true?' enquired my sister, totally lost.

'If I'm not mistaken, this is Giddeon's handwriting, my friend in Uganda. He didn't tell me he was going to be in the country any time soon.'

Then it occurred to me to check the name on the note. Lo and behold, it was his. Fear and excitement hung all over me. It was he, I concluded. He had indicated where he was in the note. We left immediately to go to his address, only to find out that he had gone out with his friend. All the hunger that had been ripping me apart disappeared. I was dying to see him. Different feelings played ping-pong within me. Time seemed to be decidedly slow.

After what seemed like ages, we finally met. I'm no archer, but I shot myself to him like an arrow on target. I could've passed through him had he not been strong enough to stop me. I didn't even know what I was doing, but I had no control over myself. For me, it was the distorted scene of *Romeo and Juliet*-with Juliet actually waking up to find Romeo alive. The effusion! He held me tight and I wanted to climb on him like an orange tree. I wished the hug from which we finally tore ourselves apart had lasted forever. Anyone looking at us would not have been totally wrong to think we were lovebirds. I couldn't get enough of him as I stepped back a little and took a look at him. He looked more mature and more handsome than before. His speech was even softer.

That evening, I invited him and his friend for dinner. When you have a special guest, you dig deeper into your pocket, and I did. We had a lengthy and pleasant conversation during dinner before he left with his friend. Before leaving, he promised to visit the following day and asked what dish I would be cooking. I told him, but then said I wasn't quite sure. The point wasn't whether I was going to cook or not; it was that I was going to have to cook cheaper food because I didn't have enough money left for the week. I wasn't ashamed but felt it important to prepare him for that.

To my surprise, he dipped his hand into his pocket and left something in my hand, asking me to add that to whatever I had on me. I'd be doing my feelings linguistic injustice if I said I was not touched. I had this rush that left me smiling in awe. It wasn't about the money-it could've come from anybody in the world. It was about where the money was coming from. From somebody who genuinely cared, it was a two-way street, I mean. It's different, so amazingly different.

I don't know if you've realised that the value of a gift is often determined by how dear the receiver holds the giver in their heart. Finally, it's about the heart, it dawned on me. He still cared. He cared even more. He could sacrifice the little he'd got for me.

God, after all these years? How do I not fall for your servant? Please, help me get out of this, I would soliloquize. I don't know if you've ever had to love that small voice in you that's dishing out the opposite prayer; I mean the real prayer, the truth you don't want to accept.

Before leaving Buea, he spent a night at my place. I might have been somewhat scared, but it turned out to be so amazing. I've got some juicy details here. I can stake my money on the fact that you're dying to hear them right now. That was the first time a man ever spent the night in my room. Be honest with me, what do you expect, when a man spends the night in the same bed with a woman he has feelings for, especially if the woman can't claim otherwise for herself?

I could feel the cosy warmth of his body as he lay down next to me. We could hear the melody from the percussion of our two hearts harmoniously playing together. The silence hung heavy in the room, even the tick of a watch could be heard very distinctly. We were both expecting something; perhaps some movement from one of us. There was no way I was going to be the one. I couldn't sleep. His breath was heavy. Just when I was about to give up, I felt his body lightly against mine. My heart loved it and thumped harder; but my head wasn't quite sure about it. I decided to listen to my heart first. I encouraged him on, giving him the green light and responding with enthusiasm. Then he was totally ready and went for...

Then he was totally ready to make love to me. What he didn't know was that I had set my limits.

'No, I can't,' I whispered.

'I thought you were ready and wanted to.'

'No,' I feigned disinterest. How could he have known I was flaming with desire inside?

This took him aback, but the struggle went on as he constantly kept nudging and making me feel his hardness against the softness of my thighs. I reluctantly gave in and was very surprised when he turned it down.

'I respect you and wouldn't want to go against your wishes. If you've said no several times, then I want to believe you know why. I'm sorry, I can't.'

I decided to give in because you insisted, I muttered to myself in an aside. Was it a test or something? If yes, had I failed or passed? What was the point? My mind went on and on, but I was grateful that he cared about my feelings. He left for Bamenda the following day.

From Bamenda, he moved on to the UK for further training and we started communicating via emails. At some point, I noticed he was changing the way he ended his letters–romance was gradually infiltrating his words. I was delighted by everything he wrote and would print out his emails so I could go through them over and over again. At some point, rumour reached me that he had been dismissed from the Mill Hill house. Part of me was mad. Another rumour said I was the cause of his dismissal. How could that have been? I might have not been perfect, but I had tried hard to keep a healthy relationship with him. When some friends came to me to ask whether he'd really been dismissed, I told them I was waiting for him to tell me that himself.

He finally gave me his reasons for leaving. I was okay with him. This did not affect our friendship in any way. His emails became frequent. However, he kept changing the way he closed his letters to me. I observed quietly as the affection went from strength to strength.

One evening in 2002, I had a phone call from him.

'What are you doing?' he asked.

'I'm just having a rest in my room.'

After some general conversations, he said he had something to ask me.

'Will you marry me?' his voice and what he was asking came like a dream to me. Marry him? I could not think straight. But I had to tell him something.

'I... Yes, I will,' I screamed into the phone.

That was somehow the most natural thing for me to say. With Gi, my heart always overpowered my head.

'It's a yes between us,' I added. 'But I'll have to discuss it with my elder sister (Matilda) first.' She has always been like a mum to me.

The shock was so big, moving straight from not becoming a priest to becoming a husband. Wasn't it too fast? What was so special about me that would push a well-travelled man to still come back to a poor girl like myself? I might have said yes from the most sacred part of my heart, but I remained worried still. I was worried about the myth that *bushfallers (a word referred to those who leave Cameroon and travel to a foreign, western country)* promised marriages to girls in Africa and ended up keeping them waiting forever while they lived away their lives abroad with different women.

It's not like I didn't trust Gi. Of course, I did. You know, a dose of what-if could be helpful sometimes. What if he wasn't the right person for me? I mean, that God-sent. What if he was already married and was just deceiving me? But why in the world would he do that? As for my parents' consent, I knew I could handle that. Gi was my choice and I truly loved him. I'd always loved him so much despite all my pathetic attempts at fighting it. Just hearing from him was like smoking weed, I always ended up high. It didn't matter what he wrote. My heart was like a drum and Gi's voice the drumstick. It didn't matter what he said. My entire being was like a marionette and Gi the marionettist. Nothing else mattered. The soft way in which he spoke made me feel like he'd got everything under control. His respect for a woman made me see myself crowned in his kingdom. I wanted my womb to house his kids; I wanted to be the one who took care of him. My fears of us not having dated before; not knowing the other side of him; and not knowing whether we would be compatible in marriage or not did matter, but I knew we were going to conquer all with love and commitment. Nothing else mattered. I believed love was enough to perfect our imperfections. I still do.

I had to break the news to my elder sister. So, I wrote her a letter telling her there was something important I needed us to discuss in person. I made sure I didn't let the cat out of the bag. Unfortunately, her mind flew in the wrong direction to fill the blank space in my letter. She was furious in her reply.

"If you've decided to become pregnant out of wedlock like the others have done, you better just stay where you are because I'm not ready to welcome a bastard child in my house", she wrote. I understood her worries perfectly well. All I did was smile after reading through her letter. I didn't bother to reassure her that it wasn't anything close to what she was thinking.

The day came and I finally travelled to Bamenda. When I told her about the proposal, she was very shocked. It was hard for me to tell whether she was relieved that her suspicions were not true or happy that someone was asking for my hand in marriage. Perhaps, both. Her shock was also partly due to the fact that the person dangling a marriage proposal in front of her kid sister was supposed to be pursuing a career as a priest. How come he now wanted to marry me? Then she said these words which I have never forgotten:

'Tell him he has given me a bitter pill to swallow.'

Bitter pill to swallow? Whatever did that mean, I knew it could only be something good. As mums and daughters or sisters will always have their little secrets, we agreed that I was going to pick a convenient time to discuss it with everyone. 'Everyone' here, referred to her husband and herself. She would have to pretend she knew nothing about it, too.

It was Easter 2002. I decided to tell everyone after Easter Vigil Mass. When I was done, the first thing her husband did was turn and ask his wife whether she knew anything about what I was saying. She, for her part, stuck to our initial agreement.

'Claris has merely informed us,' he went on. 'She didn't sound as though she was asking our opinion.' Then turning to me, he asked: 'Am I correct, Claris? 'I nodded a yes.

I had always believed that marriage is supposed to come from the heart, not from those around. No one was going to decide who I got married to. That was it gradually coming to pass. My brother-in-law wasn't done with me, yet though. Did I just say, brother-in-law? Sorry, that was a mistake. I feel more comfortable referring to him as my elder sister's husband (Georges). Just like his wife, he was like a dad to me. I know you'll agree with me it's somewhat odd to refer to a father figure as a brother-in-law. There are times when sticking to English rules and the so-called appropriate vocabulary could really make one sound boring and stupid.

'Claris, most of these guys have their lives going on where they are. There are many girls who have grown old and are still single and frustrated today because some guy abroad promised them marriage and kept them waiting. Some of them even return home married to a white lady. I'm not going to let that happen to you. No. No! I'm going to give this man six months. If he doesn't formalise this, then I'm sorry, you'll have to move on with your life. If this man could disappoint the church, then what more of you?' stated my brother-in-law.

I was broken and disappointed. How could he say that? Was he for me or against me? Why would he want to discourage me if he was for me? I later understood what he was thinking, when my emotions got out of the way. He had my interests at heart, as any right-thinking father would. With that settled, I could go on to inform the other key people in my household.

My man was already making plans to come home for the wedding before six months had passed. My sister's husband couldn't hide his surprise.

'I didn't know that your guy was serious,' he told me one day. I just smiled.

I carefully selected who to inform and discuss my marriage plans with. Most people were too pessimistic and could only say discouraging things. I avoided them. Even most of my friends had nothing good to say. I guess that's life. Would you believe it if I told you some have never spoken to me since then? While some attended the wedding as doubting Thomases, others whom I thought were really close to me did not show up at all. When I think of how it used to bother me back then, I smile at my naivety.

There was a lot of crazy gossip circulating about our wedding. So much negativity. I will not bore you with the details. What really bothered me though and I think you should know was what a certain priest, a well-meaning man, told us. He sat us down, waving his phone from side to side in a rather theatrical manner, and asked if it was only through the phone that this wedding had been discussed? Another priest, who was also a family member, made an appointment with me. When I went there he said he had something very important to discuss with me. He asked me how many siblings I have and how many does my husband have. I told him and I could not just believe what came out of his mouth. So, this priest man, asked me, if I have carefully considered the fact that I was from a large family and getting married into another large family, would not be beneficial to me at all?

You know how it goes: when it's love, it's all. That's why they say FALL IN LOVE. When you truly fall in love, it's hard to bring you down again because you're already down. It's that simple. When a relationship is based on love, there's no telling what the people involved can go through together without breaking apart. We showed a deaf ear to the naysayers, that was us. To those friends who said I was only getting married to him because I wanted to *fall bush*, they could only speak their minds but not affect mine. They thought they knew everything, but they knew next to nothing about us.

It was all a huge success. In the space of two weeks, we did the traditional wedding, the civil wedding and the church wedding. He then returned to the UK.

Where I was raised in Africa, family is everything, regardless of whether it is the nuclear or the extended family. In Kom specifically, where I'm from, as well as other tribes with which I came into contact before leaving Cameroon, riches are mostly measured in terms of one's relationship with others and their family, especially their children. Some years back, the number of wives a man had, used to be very important as it gave him prestige and earned him respect from his peers. The notion of continuity, having offspring to guarantee that one generation survives another, is paramount.

Perhaps I internalised one environment and took it to another which didn't quite correspond. Truth be told, I have grown to love and believe in these values that uphold humanity. It has always been my conviction that any other thing should be secondary to humanity if the world is to be the beautiful place we all wish it were: the humanity of our actions, the humanity of our decisions, the humanity of our plans, the humanity of our achievements, the humanity of our families, the humanity of our businesses, the humanity of our relationships, the humanity of our communities, the humanity of our world, the humanity of our humanity. How often do we think about this, let alone make it part and parcel of us? That the humanity of things should be the soul of everything we do is how I was raised. The sad news is that many of these values took the degrading shape of ideals the moment I stepped foot on English soil. That notwithstanding, I remain unapologetic for cherishing and holding tight to these values which to others might seem absurdly idealistic. That is who I am; I happen to believe in myself.

While growing up, I always knew I would someday be a mother to very handsome boys. I did not really think much about girls. But whenever I did, I would always have this image of a younger version of myself. Fate had it that I got married in 2003 and had to move to the UK. Nonetheless, it became quite complicated because securing a visa was difficult. It was during the fifth attempt that I was granted a visa. It's been REAL MARRIED LIFE since 4 November 2004 when I stepped foot on British soil. It's been love over everything else. I don't have to explain that to you, do I?

Life seemed just fine, though not as fine as I had expected. Not that I was expecting to move into a mansion or be showered with gifts, money and the rest. But life was somewhat different. Before getting married, I thought marriage was a union for two, who, after compromising, sacrificing and making the informed, yet firm decision, came to live together for the rest of their lives here on earth. I thought after such a life-changing decision, one had to leave behind so many things which one used to do while single, and even leave behind some of the relationships one had before getting married. I thought marriage was what-is-yours-is-mine and what-is-mine-is-yours. I saw marriage as an imperfect union of perfect love and of total honesty, even when it hurts. I, however, learnt that marriage is a whole new school of two illiterates.

I conceived pregnancy in matrimony as a blessing from heaven which should be gladly received and celebrated by the couple involved and jointly taken care of with love. I thought it all meant the two being able and willing to care for each other both in times of sickness and in health. The list is long.

Maybe I ended up so disappointed because I got into it with too many idealistic expectations up in my head, but I don't regret anything. Time has taught me quite a lot; the more I understand, the happier I become. Whoever said it only gets better in time can see me after this book for a drink. I still believe in doing the right thing and clinging to my expectations; I still believe in working towards them; I still believe in a universe where this is all possible. What might have changed is my approach. Where I'm from, people still care about one another; people are still their brothers' and sisters' keepers.

A few months after my arrival in the United Kingdom, I took a pregnancy test and it was positive. For those of us from Africa, you know the feeling, don't you? That overpoweringly tingly sensation of glee wrapped in a bundle of pride and sealed with a string of fulfilment by a pair of hands from heaven, dulling your rationality and leaving you in cloud nine. Then you find yourself running to him to share the good news which you believe will have him treat you like his queen, at least for a day. Yes, I couldn't wait to break the news to my king; I couldn't wait to tell him there was a prince (ss) on the way. His prince (ss), his grain, his blood. I wanted him to know my fertile womb had germinated the healthy seed he had sown and that I was going to take very good care of it so he could harvest the best fruits from the baobab I was going to grow it into. I was dying to have him give me that *you're-the-best-thing-in-my-world* look. Gooseflesh, lost in my own delusional imagination, unable to distinguish between reality and fantasy, I closed my eyes and drank in a mouthful of refreshing breath like a starved addicted cigarette smoker who has been ordered to suck on a lit cigarette just once.

But no, it was stillness and serenity. The reaction when I broke the news was rather calm and tranquil; and this was nowhere close to anything I had imagined. I felt like a switch had been turned on to take me straight from a cool summer to a bitter winter. I felt bad, even though I couldn't tell exactly why? Was it because my too-high expectations of his reaction were totally crushed or that I was unable to understand him, know what he wanted and make him happy? Was it because what appeared to me to be the very essence of marriage was not warmly received by my loving husband or that I was just being loose, naive, and overexcited? Perhaps he saw things differently and had different plans for us, I thought later.

As time passed; everything gradually fell into place. The clearer my head got, the more I understood him, or tried to. It is quite common for us to expect others to react the same way as we do when faced with a similar situation. However, we are fundamentally different and have been moulded by different experiences that are all unique in their different ways. My husband might not have been ready for a baby at that particular point in time, but he was not in any way unhappy about it. It was simply his own way of receiving the news. He was supportive all along. He never asked me to have an abortion. He stood by me and never stopped loving me. I can't pretend we have a perfect home, but we've always been strong enough to go through all the storms together and emerge victorious. He's a good man, a caring dad and a loving husband who respects me as a woman and a wife.

I was eager to watch my baby grow in me, to see my stomach stretch into a round ball and change my wardrobe from fitting to lose dresses. I watched my diet and paid very close attention to the slow changes my body was undergoing. I admired the reflex in me that always protected anything from getting anywhere close to my belly. I had to be sure it was gentle and harmless before letting it come close. The days and weeks went by, every minute swelling my heart with wishes and expectations. But then, something happened in the eighth week.

Chapter Two
Grief: How it all started

I was in severe pain (2005) after about the first eight weeks of gestation and had to rush into A&E. I think the nurses there knew exactly what the problem was, but I can't tell with certainty whether or not it was explained to me. The only thing I remember is that I sat on the toilet and a lump of blood dropped into the toilet bowl. Scared and worried, I immediately called the nurses. When they came, they said something which I didn't quite get. They booked an early scan for me the following Monday at Frimley Park Hospital. The result was...bad, unfortunately. There were hormonal signs that I was pregnant; but there was no foetus in my womb. That was when it dawned on me that the lump that had dropped in the toilet bowl the other day was the foetus that had been in my womb. So, that was a miscarriage, my heart wept. How could my first pregnancy end up like that? All the hopes I had been nursing, all the dreams I had been fondling, all the happiness I had been cuddling and all the fulfilment in which I had been cushioned were all squeezed out through my lacrimal ducts in a matter of seconds.

It felt like a nightmare in which I was stuck and couldn't snap out of it into real life. I cried and cried but did not know who to talk to. I don't know if I even wanted to talk to anybody. The truth remains, however, that I was not referred for help in any form. That was it, like a fleeting thought, a baby had gone.

I remember mentioning it to a priest (Father) in my church and asking for a special mass intention, but I never had the opportunity to grieve this baby. Maybe I was never given the chance because, after that day, no one ever talked about that baby since. I understand it can be quite a sensitive and difficult topic to talk about, but it happened. Why on earth do we have to act as though it never happened?

I hope I don't get misunderstood as trying to invite self-pity upon myself. No, far from that, the loss of a baby, no matter how young, hurts just as much. It is okay for me to grieve if that makes me feel better. To this day, for some strange reason, I still strongly believe it was a girl. I hope you don't take it personally when I say I still miss her.

Several weeks after, I was asked to book an appointment with the doctor, so I could be put on contraceptive pills as Giddeon was not quite sure if he was ready for a baby. I did as I was instructed, although that wasn't quite what I wanted, but it wasn't all about me. I compromised and went to the doctors who prescribed me some pills.

The pills were useless, however, because I was already pregnant with Lesra before I could start taking them. My husband received the news in his usual peaceful and measured approach. This time around, I tried to understand him, and not let his attitude bother me, but over the years, I have given serious thought to this and so many other things that transpired.

Lesra's pregnancy was quite eventless for 6 months. There were no issues until 1 October 2005. I did not sleep well that night. I got up at some point and sat at the edge of the bed, then got up to go to the toilet. When I came back, I discovered it was a bit wet where I had sat at the edge of the bed. It did not occur to me that something was amiss. I thought it was normal to go through such moments just the same as it was to feel tired, listless, etc. For breakfast, I decided to eat beans (red kidney beans). But when it was ready, I put mine out on a plate and then put it back in the microwave to reheat. I added a pinch of pepper to the very hot food and ate it just as hot as it was. I had lost my sense of taste, so I needed very hot and spicy food, just to see if I was going to regain my appetite

On 1 October, we all went for a christening ceremony. While at the reception, I felt tired and listless. The world around me looked bland and insipid. All of a sudden, a Nigerian lady of blessed memory (RIP) asked Giddeon to take me home because she could sense that I was not quite well. I was shocked because she hadn't asked me how I was feeling, and I hadn't told her anything. I remember going to the toilet and my discharge was a bit like chocolate. It was a relief for me when Giddeon took me home before going back to rejoin the celebrations.

About 30 minutes afterwards, I started suffering from stomach aches and cramps. Then I went to the toilet and discovered I was bleeding a little. That was when I called Giddeon and Pius (one of our friends) who came and took me to the hospital. They examined me and found out that I was fully dilated and had been in labour for about 24 hours. Needless to say, I was shocked and devastated.

'Sorry, Madam, you will soon be having your baby,' said the doctor.

'I'm still 24 +5 weeks pregnant, remember,' I whispered to the doctor.

It was already too late, though. I was a young 28-year-old, who'd had one miscarriage and not fully recovered from and was about to have a baby at just 24 weeks gestation in a foreign land (from Cameroon) with neither relations nor friends.

I couldn't tell whether it was my body that was still or the world around me that had stood still. Crying as I did, only made me more helpless than before. That was when I turned to God and handed Him the situation. With my Rosary, I prayed that God would reverse the situation. Somewhere in my heart, I knew that any baby born before eight or nine month's gestation would never survive. This made me mourn my baby before giving birth to him.

Mine and the baby's heartbeats were being monitored. Suddenly, at about 1:50 a.m. my waters broke and baby Lesra was born exactly 4 minutes afterwards. Given that I was dizzy after inhaling the gas and air, I dosed off and Lesra was immediately whisked away for resuscitation. I was very certain that would be the end of him. Giddeon came back a couple of hours later and assured me Lesra was fine. He was taken to the intensive care unit, however, as he was just too small to breathe on his own. Once he'd been intubated and all the necessary cannulas put on him, I was wheeled to see him. When I placed my little finger into his palm, he grabbed it and that was the love, the bond that has always glued us beyond just mum and son. When Lesra reads this, this will be the first time he will have a better understanding about his birth and what we've been through together.

The story and experience with Lesra is another story for another time, which will obviously be another book, but for now, let us see what happened as the years went by.

With the experience I'd had with miscarriage and premature birth, it was only natural that I was worried about having another premature baby if I fell pregnant again. Once one has given birth to a preemie or has experienced a high-risk pregnancy, the decision to have another child can be very difficult or quite daunting. You wonder if your next pregnancy will be as difficult or as risky as the previous. You wonder if you'll have another child in the NICU (Neonatal Intensive Care Unit), or if you'll have to face another loss. There are emotional risks, financial risks, and sometimes traumatic effects. While a previous premature birth does make it more likely that you'll have another premature baby, this isn't always the case. Many women whose first child was premature, go on to have their next baby at full-term like it occurred in my case.

I had my second baby at just at 24 weeks + 5 days gestation. It was a time of a roller coaster of emotions. It was so unexpected. Exactly 4.5 years afterwards, we decided it was time to try for another baby. There was obviously the fear of having this next baby early, losing him or even my life, but at the same time, it's difficult to predict the future of a pregnancy even if it's all healthy in the beginning. Anything can still go wrong at some point.

When I finally took off my coil, we were both surprised at how quickly I got pregnant, since normally it's believed that if one has been on the coil for a long period, then it takes time for the person to fall pregnant again once it's removed. But this time around, it wasn't the case. Somehow, we were not really completely prepared emotionally or psychologically or even financially. Our plan was that after the coil was taken out and my body was getting ready, we would also be discussing what to do and what not to do given the previous preterm birth, while trying for the baby. But it appears baby had his own plans (which that is usually the case with me; very easy to fall pregnant but at risk of having the baby early or even so early, there's risk of death).

Whilst pregnant, I literally counted from day 1 till when the baby was born. Because of the fear that I may end up having another preterm baby, I was frequently stressed, having lots of mood swings and constantly crying. I also forgot that stress alone could lead to another preterm birth. My heart felt like it was always held in my hands all the time. But the one thing that kept me going was the baby who kept growing and this reassured me. Also, I had to be regularly seen by an obstetrician/gynaecologist so that my cervix could be checked and measured in case it stared dilating and for baby to be monitored regularly as my pregnancy was considered a high risk. This wasn't an easy journey but we pulled through it as a family. Baby kept growing and I kept glowing even though due to constant stress and worries, I had a huge breakout of acne both on my face and on my back but that was the least of my worries. It was an amazing journey, one full of ups and downs, being pregnant and taking care of my son, who has additional needs. How I pulled through, only God alone knows.

Amazingly, I ended up having a full 40-week pregnancy. Apparently, the young man was so comfortable in my tummy that he didn't want to be born and so he extended his belly stay for another 4 days.

Finally, labour had to be induced. It lasted for about 13 hours. In the end, it was discovered that, labour took so long because baby's hand was wrapped around his neck. Thank

God for a keen and careful midwife (whom I've never met since then).

Even though it was a long and tiring labour, I finally laid eyes on my beautiful bouncing baby boy, weighing 3.98kg. It was so overwhelming to see him, feel him and even hear him cry for the first time in his life. Something I'd never previously experienced; to have a full-term baby and being able to hear the baby cry and also knowing that in 2 or 3 days, I was going to be taking my baby home. All hell broke loose at those thoughts: thoughts of; whether I was going to cope with caring for another baby with the first one having special needs.

I cried and cried, and the midwife was surprised. I'd got a bouncy, healthy baby in my arms, so why should I be crying. So, my husband explained to her that I was just shedding tears of joy because that was my first time having a full-term baby. When I finally brought him home, I used to physically check on Ankini while he was sleeping to make sure he was okay and breathing properly. Unfortunately, that's what I used to do with his big brother just to make sure he was breathing and was still alive because he was on home oxygen for the first 2 years of his life. So, subconsciously, I started doing the same with Ankini until one day, my mum stopped me halfway on my way to his room. She told me that the baby is okay and that she understood what was happening and she reassured me that all was fine. Maybe I just needed that reassurance.

As the years went by, Ankini has been so special to me, the same as my other children. He is a very kind little lad, even though sometimes he can be a hand full.

As Ankini has been growing up, he notices how different his brother is. He notices his difficulties and he has asked so many questions. There are times he really wants to play properly with Lesra but Lesra is autistic with severe learning disabilities and additional needs, he struggles with communication, imagination and interactions with others. So, when Ankini turned 7 years old, he started asking about a younger brother and saying he wanted someone who would be able to call him big brother. He said he was tired of being called little brother all the time. So, he started asking me when I was going to have a little brother for him.

I cannot tell if falling pregnant unexpectedly was Ankini's answer to his prayers of having a younger brother. While I was pregnant, Ankini was so excited. He wanted to tell everyone that he was going to have a little brother, and he was heartbroken when my pregnancy didn't end the way we anticipated it would. He was sad, he was angry that he had to now tell his friends that he was no longer going to be having a baby brother. He also said to me at some point that he was ashamed.

You must be wondering who Davi –Jayce is. Let me tell you about him.

Waters broken for four days! Baby still breathing, coming slowly, gradually fighting and pushing through the thick walls of the vagina with foot first. Life. Fighting for his life. I want to stretch an arm and yank his tender innocent body into the safety of my arms of love. To cuddle him while he melodiously chants into my ears. Stroke his sleek light hair with all the care left in my soul. Tell him how impatiently his dad, Lesra, Ankini and I have been waiting to cradle, smell and love him. Oh, my sweet Davi-Jayce! I might have hugged and cuddled him a thousand and one times in my imagination, my face creasing into a smile while I heaved a healing sigh every time such therapeutically overpowering images sneaked into my head and ordered my heart to pump faster. Love. Davi-Jayce, that's love. Pure love. Feeling you play with me from my womb with those mum-I-will-soon-be-with-you kicks. Yes, D-J knows just how much I love him and can reciprocate that with his kicks. D-J can't wait to come home. It's barely 22 weeks gone, D-J. It is true we can't wait to hug you, too. But we were hoping you would stay a little longer. The doctors say it's a bit too early, but my boy is on his way and I want to have him. Somewhere deep in the back of my mind, I try to suppress the unanswered question that keeps lingering in my head while nibbling away at my heart: why is my body rejecting my baby this much?

Waters broken first. And then, his cute little leg is stuck between my legs. The doctors try to help, giving me options. Options? I don't know about options; I know about my baby. It's either I have my baby or I have my baby. Don't you see him fighting? Please, he's blood of my blood and flesh of my flesh. God! I know you can do this for me. The doctors may be thinking that D-J wants to leave. They're right, he wants to leave my womb so he can live in my arms; not leave the world as their eyes coldly message to me. Pains? No way! You should understand I'm numb to that. The fear of losing my boy is bigger than that of sharing the same bed with a boa. He is the life of my life and I wouldn't mind sacrificing mine so the me in him gets to see the light of day. Just let me reincarnate in him if that's what it takes for him to live. You probably think I'm mad, don't you? Well, just in case I forgot to tell you, I'm equally numb to your thoughts. D-J, hold on my boy, we can do this. Yes, mum is a fighter, too. You think it's hard for me, don't you? Well, it's even harder for D-J. Think about him: his bag of protective fluid is all gone. He's dry in there while his leg hangs out here, living in two separate worlds at the same time. I can't pretend to imagine what you are going through in there. How dare they act as though it were all about me? That they don't see you gnashing your teeth and clenching your fists does not mean your fragile body is not wracked by pain.

But wait, maybe I should tell you how I encountered Ancheitiimbom Davi-Jayce.

It was 5 May 2017. I sat on that Princes House toilet seat holding an already used pregnancy test strip firmly in both of my hands with my eyes closed. For some strange reason, part of me wanted positive while the other wanted negative. Anxiety ripped me apart as I impatiently waited to know the truth. You know that deep feeling of hating something you don't yet know? I still don't understand why I did not like a result I was yet to find out. Lord, negative, negative, make this negative, I prayed in silence. Fortunately, and unfortunately, there was a thick blue cross indicating high levels of pregnancy hormones. Yes, I was already 2-3 weeks into pregnancy. I felt as though it was all a dream from which I was going to snap out of. How could I be pregnant? It was hard for me to embrace the thought of a baby forming in my womb. Quietly, I despairingly cried in the silence of the room, which only seemed to mock at me. I felt dejected. Don't be alarmed, please. It's not like I honestly did not want this baby. Of course, I could not have been ungrateful for this gift of the womb. A baby is a gift from God and the coming of one into the universe should leave dimples in our hearts. The tears were for different reasons: first, I was not actively trying for a baby; second, I did not ask for him. So, it goes without saying that I was not psychologically and financially prepared for one.

Lord, why now? I found myself asking. God's ways are obviously different from ours. Sometimes, God answers past requests for reasons mortals like us may not fathom. His calendar is different from ours and His timing perfect, even when we don't understand Him. With these thoughts crowded on my mind, I felt firmly ensconced in a strong current of boundless energy. I felt nestled in the mystery of His love.

With tear-stained cheeks, I still managed to forge a smile, which I always do. That was when I started seeing how blessed I was. Reasons to be happy flooded my mind in thousands. What about those many women out there who have tried for a baby for so many years, using all possible means to conceive to no avail, I thought. How about those with the ability and will to spend any amount of money or use any means conceivable to man so they could get pregnant? There was I, seriously crying and grieving because I had a positive test in my hand. My grief was short-lived as it soon gave way to an all-pervading sense of guilt.

I pray my crying should not be misunderstood as hate for my baby. God forbid! My crying was due to my past experiences, challenges and struggles with the other pregnancies I'd had. I have never had any difficulties with conceiving or in trying for a baby. I was in a dilemma of whether to keep this baby or not. I had to carefully think this through and fervently pray over it. Wasn't it just a few weeks ago I had told a friend about how careful I had to be not to get pregnant? I had expressed my fears and uncertainty about keeping the baby if that happened. Was this a trial or something? The baby was already forming in me without my consent and without any signs, yet. In the depth of my confusion, a calm voice suddenly broke into my brooding solitude:

Look Claris, where have you kept your faith? God has a reason for everything. Get up, wipe your tears and go back into that office and cry no more for God gives when He wants.

These thoughts continued to echo in my head even when I had gone back into the office and was sat at my desk. Then, this small quiet voice in my head started analysing the whole situation:

You are married; you're a strong and brave woman. You're energetic and capable of so many things given your past experiences. You have to choose between these two scenarios and, whichever you opt for, be ready to face the consequences for the rest of your life:

1. *Do you want to get rid of this baby just because you are broke? It was not planned, and you are afraid you won't cope with the challenges that come with childbearing based on your past experiences with your other children. Are you ready to spend the rest of your life regretting and feeling guilty for getting rid of an innocent baby?*

2. *Alternatively, do you want to embrace, accept, love and cherish this baby, knowing fully well that there will be challenges and difficulties which will eventually come to pass someday?*

As the voice in my head drew to an end, I smiled to myself and opted for the latter. Challenges, difficulties and struggles will always come to an end, I told myself, but guilt might hunt you for the rest of your life. Thinking again, I remembered that when God puts one in a difficult situation, in an unplanned or unknown journey, He doesn't abandon them there. He gives them a roadmap to guide them all the way. One has to bear in mind that no child has ever chosen the circumstances under which they are conceived or in which they will be born. It could be planned or unplanned, in marriage or out of wedlock, etc. Once it happens, we have to learn to embrace and accept and love them unconditionally.

Now you know how I first met one of my sweethearts, Ancheitiimbom Davi-Jayce. I always fondly call him D-J; but there's more you wouldn't want to miss, trust me.

Perhaps I have no idea what you are going through, but it crushes my soul to know your innocent body (D-J) is wracked by pain. You might have been a surprise in my womb, but I've grown to smile at the thought of falling asleep and waking up with a bigger you in me. A bigger you and a bigger bundle of love, reflecting with radiating suppleness that commands admiration from the outside. It hurts to watch you hurt; but it hurts, even more, to be helpless before the silence of your pains. Mothers are supposed to be natural lifesavers. God, I pray I don't fail you D-J.

You see, when a doctor gives a mother options around death, it's a feeling like having your heart ripped out of your chest and placed on the road for a truck to crush it. How on earth do you expect me to subscribe to one of your options around death? Love looks past the thick walls of impossibilities; love prays and looks for ways to make it work; love hangs on and keeps hopes green even in the face of the deadliest of storms; love sacrifices. No matter what, love doesn't know death as an option. In all my pains, all I see is your soft body in my arms as I hear your sweet cry caress my soul. D-J, please hang on, we can do this.

I picture D-J on the verge of falling off a cliff with only my little finger for him to hold on to and be saved. He must hang in there while I do my best to force my frail body to pick him up. It's a rocky top, a rocky cliff and a rocky bottom. The muscles of our flesh are breaking away and dying off, but we are growing the muscles of our faith and hope. We both depend on one another for this to work. If he falls, I fall with him. I don't know how, but D-J must not slip off. Can you picture the bloody beads of sweat on my forehead dripping off on the stiffness of his strained and rigid body? He's my hero and heroes don't go down like that. They fight. Do you now have a clue of our plight and how far we are ready to go to pull this off? No, I doubt if you do, but go tell the doctor we need him to believe in us.

We need him to do better. He can't give up on us now. Tell the doctor 22 weeks is full life and if it is life then it can be saved. Remind the doctor he has no idea how many times D-J and I have played together in my mind and the spiritual bond that links us together. D-J and I have plans; plans to change the world and make it a better place; plans to hug ourselves and be happy. Dad has fatherly plans for little D-J. Lesra and Ankini have their brotherly plans, too. So much depends on D-J. Tell the doctor we need more than his best.

I hope you (reader) don't mind if I steal into your time a bit and explain the events leading to the bursting of my baby's amniotic fluid at barely 22-weeks into our journey. Well, I guess I'm the boss here, the one in the driving seat, so you just have to sit tight and ride along.

2 September 2017 was a bright and sunny Saturday and the temperature was about 20°C. I couldn't really say why, but I didn't feel like leaving the house anymore. I had prepared fish to be roasted for the meeting at midday, but I ended up yielding to the incomprehensible inertia and not going to the meeting after all. I wasn't in any form of pain, though. I could not say exactly what the problem was. I just felt listless and had no interest in anything (a feeling similar to the one I had just before I was rushed to hospital before having Lesra)

On Monday 4th, I discovered I had more vaginal discharge, was overcome by dizziness and could feel some pain in my lower back. I booked an appointment with the doctors. It was on this day I was told my iron levels were a bit low. Swabs were done; the baby's heart rate was checked, and everything seemed to be just fine.

The following day, I did not go to work. It was InSeT (In-service Training) day at school, so Ankini was off. We went to the shopping centre and visited KFC (Kentucky Fried Chicken) where we had lunch. Though I had been suffering from a lack of appetite throughout the pregnancy, I noted that it was a bit worse that day. From that day on, for some strange reason, I started leaving the house with two handbags: one with my maternity notes in and the other for work or other outings.

On Tuesday 5th, I went for the blood tests as well as for occupational health checks. The blood tests indicated that I was slightly anaemic, so I was put on iron tablets. On Wednesday 6th, I went to work, and everything still felt alright. At about 4 a.m. on Thursday 7th, I went to urinate and, on getting back to bed, I felt a little trickle of water down my thigh. I immediately thought I had not wiped myself well after urinating. With that in my head, I calmly went to bed. Just before leaving the house for work the following day, I went to the toilet as usual to move my bowels. As I relieved myself, I felt as though something inside me had shifted downwards. However, I couldn't tell what it was. I rushed downstairs and quickly googled early signs of cervix dilation. I found out that about three of the signs I had been having were on the list. At this point, a tiny voice laced with uncertainty echoed deep in me and said that I should take a day off from work and go to my usual Basingstoke hospital for a check-up, just in case there was something amiss.

On second thoughts, I reassured myself that I worked at Royal Berkshire Hospital and could just walk into Accident and Emergency (A&E) for a consultation if anything went wrong. Wrapped in the soothing warmth of this consoling thought, I left for work like I would have done on any other day. However, this poorly justified consolation was rather short-lived. As I drove to work, my mind kept taking me back to what I had felt in the morning. Truth be told, this is one of those moments that always still sneak up on me and nibble away at my peace of mind; one of those moments that send shudders down my spine when my mind's eye hits the rear view of my life; one of those moments that leave me cringing and empty, wishing that I could go back in time and save a hunch from a punch.

The morning kept replaying as I drove on. I arrived at my workplace just a few minutes before 10 a.m. Given that I had to go for training that morning, I decided to go to the toilet first. Lo and behold, there was an alarming sign that looked rather unpleasant to me. During pregnancy, the expectant mother is not really supposed to experience any signs of blood when passing urine. This was the alarming sign that I spotted on wiping myself. I suppressed the urge to have my devastated self, create a scene and willed myself to walk back into the office where I took my car keys and, in a semblance of calmness, walked out as though I was headed for the training. I went and got my emergency handbag from the car before continuing to the A&E (Accident & Emergency).

'We're just going to run a few checks on you here at A&E, after which we will send you back to your own hospital,' a nurse told me. 'Given that you're not booked at RBH (Royal Berkshire Hospital), we can't see you at the assessment unit.'

So, I pleaded with them to book an ambulance to take me to my hospital and was told the doctor would see into that at A&E. Observations were done and they said everything seemed fine at the moment. It suddenly dawned on me that something was definitely wrong when I went for a urine sample. I was terribly furious and presented the sample bottle as it was to the nurse in order to make sure that she understood what I was talking about. Without further waste of time, she called the doctor and pleaded with him to attend to me immediately because what she had in front of her was not a pretty sight. The doctor came without delay and, after conducting a check on me, sent me to the Day Assessment Unit (DAU) for a speculum examination. In a sorrowful ripple of echo, 'I-am-sorry,' intermittently trailed off in my ears as I was in a semblance of a trance. These words immediately jogged my memory back to 1 October 2005 when I was informed I was soon going to have Lesra after I had unknowingly been in labour for 24 hours.

As those words kept echoing in my head, I suddenly said, 'But the cervix can be stitched.'

'I'm sorry,' the midwife repeated, 'there had been a leak at the back of the membrane. It is already too late.'

I then excused myself and went to the toilet. Lo and behold, like a pierced water-filled hot air balloon, all my waters broke and the floor was a sea in the middle of which I stood, lost, my spirits drowning me deep down at the bottom as my gaze hit the opaque bleakness of the walls of nothingness. I felt as though all the blood in my body had been forced out through a single pore in just one deadly, yet painless squeeze. My legs trembled as I swung between dreaming the moment and actually living it. As the grim reality of the whole situation gradually and painfully dawned on me, I thought someone was pouring water down my spine. Did it really matter whether I accepted the fact that it was my amniotic fluid flowing out or not? Perhaps it didn't but swallowing the truth just as crude as it was, made suicide look like child's play. I can't quite remember exactly how, but my legs trembled into a wobble and gave way for my heavy body to collapse and sink into the pool.

I wailed like an abandoned child, imploring the fluid to stop flowing. I wished that the fluid would listen to my plea and not flow out; I prayed that just a bit remained so my baby could stay in there for just a few more weeks. But there was this callous deafness around me that only mocked back at my despair. In some sort of reflex, my watery and lethargic eyes scanned around the room for a container which could be used to catch the fluid and later refill it in my womb so the baby could stay in there longer. Blood was pumping so hard in my head that I felt as though the world was going to explode at any moment. My stomach churned in shock like the angry waves of a confused sea.

I did not realise that somebody had come in, but I suddenly felt the warmth of another human being against the coldness of my shrivelled body. A midwife, nurse and a healthcare assistant helped me off the floor and changed me into a hospital gown. I was then wheeled to Willows Ward, which is a quiet and comfortable room specifically allocated for parents who are about to lose their babies. It was at this point that I was told that I might have my baby at any time. However, since I was not in active labour, the pregnancy was either going to be terminated or conservative management was going to be observed until I would go into labour and have the baby naturally. I naturally opted for the latter, given that I couldn't have agreed that a baby actively moving in me be terminated. Regular observations (Obs) or vital signs were done, with bloods taken and everything still seemed just fine. The funniest part of it all was that I was still not in any form of physical pain. However, I was put on antibiotics. As my waters had gone, there was already a leak at the back of the membrane and, coupled with the baby's gestational period, I was told that there would be no plans to revive the baby after delivery. As a result, I was left with two options:

- Termination of pregnancy by induction of labour.

or

- Conservative management where Mother Nature would be allowed to take her course (so that I would go into labour naturally).

The latter being my decision, I was then admitted to Iffley Ward for further observations and where I would wait for an ambulance to take me to my local hospital. There was still no signs of infection or labour. Despite the plans in place to transfer me to my hospital, it turned out there was neither an ambulance to take me there nor a midwife to accompany me. I was made to understand that it was not an emergency. Whatever that meant, I closed my eyes and took a deep breath which brought no relief. Fleeting thoughts like a panorama of fast-forwarded images streamed through my head in a jumble, yet I had no idea what I was thinking about.

D-J keeps jogging my memory to and fro, I hope you understand that. He and I have come a long way, believe me, but the last few days have been quite tough for us. I feel like we've been caught in this for as far back as I can remember. Of course, I would someday like to recount all this to him.

At about 4:30 p.m. on 9 September, I was discharged from RBH. I still doubt whether it was right for them to do so. We arrived home at 5:30 p.m. give or take. Shortly after supper, I felt something moving down in my stomach when I visited the toilet. Then I felt with my hand, something which I was

convinced was the baby's head. As a result, we immediately
left for the hospital. I called the hospital and they asked me to
go directly to the delivery suite where I was examined and
told it was the baby's leg that was coming out instead of his
head. That was when it occurred to me that the baby was
breeched. I was then taken to the Butterfly Suite, a quiet and
comfortable room similar to the Willow Ward at RBH (where
families expecting a stillborn baby or a baby which is
expected to die during or shortly after birth) are taken.
Observations were done. Doctors attended to me and
repeated the same options that I had been given at RBH. Of
course, I still, without any hesitation, opted for conservative
management. However, I could feel baby's foot out this time.

You know what that means? Greater risk of me having an
infection, hence risking both my life and D-J's, it's that
simple. That's how we got here; and now we're stuck here. I
may be somewhat scared of what the outcome of this will
look like, but I'm praying and hoping for the best. I can't tell
you how long baby will be in there; I may not be able to tell
you just how much longer my heart will go on, but I know
for sure that my mind can't be warped. Never in my life
have I felt this right. The only fear I have left is that of losing
you (D-J), a fear that has made death non-existent.

The ward looked still and cramped and with my stale
thoughts, I felt as though I was asphyxiated. I occasionally
pulled the white sheets lightly, then place a hand on my
belly, wishing I had the superpower to will myself and D-J
out of the incomprehensible web in which we were
entangled. Here we were, stuck on the fast-breaking string
between life and death, when the string finally breaks, you
either get to live with me or in me. The doctors were selling
the latter and I the former, visualising myself kissing D-J.

I was talking to him through my mind, willing him to survive:

I want more; I want both: for you to live with me and in me. There's a home for you in my heart which can never go unoccupied, no matter what. It had always been there waiting for you to activate it with your presence in my womb. Only you had the activation code and there's no way on earth anyone, not even you, can ever deactivate it once activated. The home can only be desolate (God forbid!) but never deserted. Out here, my frail arms are cushioned and muscled with love to protect and always stand by you in the midst of all the hush, rush, slush and crush of this crazy, yet amazingly beautiful world.

Do you remember Lesra who always looked at you with those tender eyes of love through my tense round belly? Perhaps I forgot to mention to you that he and I equally had to fight through a similar complication. If Lesra and I could make it against all the odds, then we have every right to keep on fighting. All the doctors and nurses in the world may think it's over, but we can't let that get to us. They see through the eyes of science, limited science, I dare say. But we, you and I, see through the eyes of science and faith. I can't pretend to have the slightest clue of what you are going through in there, but I believe in a future with all five of us in the picture. Not only will your presence and grace adorn this picture, it will also make it even bigger and complete. Keep your eyes on the bigger picture, D-J: the family, the world.

Ancheitiimbom Davis-Jayce, you can't forget your name and what it says. You can't forget that God shields, Ancheitiimbom. We're under His wings; we're in His shelter: we can make it out of this storm unscathed. God covers everything in every home, in every family, in every situation. Though families may never be perfect, I believe my little boy has been sent to me by God for special reasons. Trust in the Lord and you will be healed. Isn't it He who covers every problem in every home? I believe my little boy is an angel sent by God to help cover these problems and shield us as a family.

There's no way I'm going to mourn another baby before his birth. I once did; it was a bitter experience; but that's all water under the bridge. I won't give myself the chance to be squashed again by a similar regret. Come what may, I have resolved to hold on to the little life left in him for as long as it can hold itself.

It's a miracle that I'm still alive and that your foot is stuck out here while your body flames up in there. It's a miracle that I still feel this strong and ready to go very much further for you and with you. That I'm not drained of life yet; that I'm not stripped of faith yet; that I haven't given in to the doctors, it's a miracle. Couldn't these miracles lead to an even bigger miracle? The Davi-Jayce Miracle, we could call it, because you've made me a believer, I look forward to seeing your miracle manifest.

God, you're our bedrock. I know there's a point to all this traumatising suspense and pain even though I may not be able to explain. I wish I could hack into your mind so I could know how this will all end up, but even if I did have the power to hack into your mind and know the outcome, I would still not trade this process for anything in the world. D-J, you're worth it. You're worth my tears and headaches; my time and my life, because God is still saying something, does it really matter what mortals are saying? I don't mean any disrespect for our doctors, D-J. All I'm saying is that it's not over, yet. So, we can't say die.

It is 10 September and everything seems to be just fine as far as the observations are concerned. Unfortunately, though, my inflammatory markers have started rising, indicating some form of infection. As a result, it's now clear that doctors will have to go against my wish for conservative management, given that I am still not in active labour. I am worried about my baby's life. So, I ask the doctors if they are still not going to revive him no matter how long he breathes. I want to know because there is still hope somewhere inside me. I insist and even call one of the hospitals reputed for caring for children born very early. Still, I'm given that same old depressive response: 'a 22-weeker is a bit too small for us to save.'

One of the midwives (Jess) who seems to have sensed my steely determination and how far I am ready to go to save my baby asks me if I want a second opinion. So, I say yes, without even thinking. Just anything that can give me some glimmer of hope is welcome.

'Are you serious?' she asks, amazed I would go to such lengths.

'Yes, I am,' I say more loudly and with force.

'I have never seen a woman as brave as you,' she finally notes.

This is just natural; I don't see anything brave in me fighting for my child. Should it be bravery as she says, then I have no exact idea about where I'm plucking it from. Maybe love, the deep unconditional and undying maternal love. I just feel like there's no bullet I wouldn't take for D-J. If you must die, then it should be in my arms, or we die together. I need you to survive and grow in my arms.

Southampton Hospital and St. George Hospitals are called, but the answer is no. I keep on insisting there must be something they can do.

'Would you like to speak to the Head of Paediatrics?'

'Yes,' I responded.

She comes and we have a long chat about the reasons a 22-week preemie baby cannot be resuscitated and why it is difficult for it even if it survived and lived.

'It is clear that your waters broke four days into the twenty-first week of pregnancy,' she goes on. 'The baby has been in you without any form of protection. So, we can't tell how much damage has already been done to the baby's lungs, let alone his brain. Besides, managing such an infant would be difficult given that there are not many hospitals sufficiently equipped to deal with such very fragile cases, and, assuming that we succeeded, we are not sure if it would have a good quality of life. That notwithstanding, every single baby is different.'

Every single baby is different? I think. It seems as though that is the only thing I have heard. My baby is definitely different, I try to convince myself. At this point, I can feel that there is something wrong because the colour of the discharge has already changed, and I am feeling ill.

'I'm afraid we may have to go against your decision of conservative management and terminate the pregnancy,' one of the medical personnel says.

The decision may still not be mine to make, but how do I digest this gloomy decision of death? Not after all this fight. How on earth do they expect me to give up now? I may have no choice now, but I still have the energy to fight their decision to decide for me. Nonetheless, they still look just as helpless and repeat that there is no way to save him. Then I ask them to explain to me what exactly they mean when they talk of termination.

'Termination at this stage involves two protocols. First, you'll have to take a tablet to kill the baby (stop his heart rate) and, second, we'll insert another tablet to induce labour (Misoprostol).'

God forbid! How do I live afterwards with the knowledge that I willingly took a tablet to terminate D-J's life? I have to do something.

Then something comes to my mind. I decide to initiate another discussion, though I am already feeling drained of energy and hope. I am administered an antibiotic infusion and paracetamol to reduce my temperature.

'If the first tablet does not induce labour, why am I supposed to take it?' I ask.

'Your baby is not going to be resuscitated. So, it does not matter.'

What? Do they have any idea what I am ready to go through for this baby? This insensitivity in this answer makes me feel like strangling someone. How can they say such a thing?

'I would very much like to have my baby alive since you have refused to resuscitate him,' I tell the doctor. 'I am not going to take the first tablet since it does not induce labour. I will have my baby alive.'

'I hope you understand that it is no guarantee that you are going to have your baby alive. You're putting us at a difficult position right now,' says the doctor.

'I just want my baby alive,' I insisted.

Maybe I feel weak, but I have to be firm on what I want. This is about me, about us. The decisions I make now will determine how I get to face life in the future. If giving up my life is the price to have him alive, then so be it.

It is clear that the doctors are afraid for my health. They have to do everything possible to save my life and I am grateful for that. Even more importantly though, I need them to do even more to save D-J's. Confused, the doctor looks up and down and then when he realises how adamant I am, he says:

'Claris, you're an incredible woman, but as it stands now, you're making this very hard for us. This procedure is the legal way and there is no way we are going to change it now. I am going to speak to my colleagues and get back to you.'

Time seems to stand still while I grow weaker. He returns after about an hour and sits by my bed.

'We will skip the first protocol,' he says, looking at me. 'I cannot assure you that you're going to have your baby alive because we cannot tell how long labour will last given that your baby has been in you without any fluid or any form of protection. So, apart from the first protocol, the plan in the documents will still be the same. Remember, I can't assure you that the baby will be born alive.'

Whether this works or not, I will remain grateful that we at least tried to give him the chance to be born alive and to let nature take its course. I don't even know if I will survive this or not. Faith is all I have now. Rising and falling faith, I mean.

So, there is an agreement that I am going to be given only the labour-inducing tablet, which is normally the second tablet to be taken in this protocol. I now have to take matters into my own hands and be in control. My midwife and I agree that I will take a bath, that after the bath, I will wear my hospital gown the other way round, getting ready to cuddle the baby. Consent forms are signed, and medication is inserted at about 4 a.m. on 11 September.

With the help of the music I have been listening to since I was admitted, I cope very well without any pain relief during labour. So, I monitor the contraction patterns and know exactly when the next one is due. Since baby's leg is already out, a bowl is placed on the toilet seat for me to use whenever I go to relieve myself. At about 11:20 a.m. I revisit the restroom and feel like the baby has shifted. As I look down, I realise both of his legs are out and can be seen. I wait for the next contraction and push immediately I feel them. Behold, I feel this rush of glee as baby gently slips out into my hands and into the bowl. Without wasting time, I immediately ring the emergency and the midwife runs in. Yes, baby is small as I look at him; but fully formed and every body part is intact. His eyes are still fused together, which is expected at this stage of gestation.

I can't stop myself from dreaming and hoping. I wonder if he will survive if he is given the chance; I still don't understand if they have concrete reasons for not resuscitating babies younger than 24 weeks. Could it be that they are just afraid of the cost? Looking at D-J, you will find it hard to imagine how difficult it would be to find a vein in his body, let alone imagine the size of the cannula that would be used. But on second thought, how come D-J survived for up to 4 days without any fluid around him? After these thoughts, I ask the midwife to check his heart rate. A doctor is also called in to confirm that Baby is still breathing. Yes, I punch an imaginary fist in the air. Baby has a heart rate and I ask for him to be placed on my chest for kangaroo care so that both I and his dad could cuddle him until he takes his last breath since they have refused to resuscitate him. D-J coughs twice while on my chest and again through my mind I speak to him:

Davi-Jayce, my son! As I hold you in my hands, I can feel your warmth, a warmth which makes me feel like squeezing you tightly. You are absolutely gorgeous, with your tongue sticking out while you suck it like your elder brother, Ankini (Born May 2010) your carbon copy, used to do.

We cuddle for a while. Then I hand him to his dad, as I did while trying to push out the placenta and was lost in the midst of excruciating pain and blood loss and when I unconsciously glanced over at Giddeon cuddling his little boy. At that moment, I could only imagine what was on his mind. I could see pain; I could see hurt and lots of unasked questions on his mind. He struggled very hard to hold his tears back. However, he was the only one who could tell exactly how he felt while holding his little D-J, I believe it was something like this:

As your father, it is natural for me to reassure you. To tell you, through this father and son tight yet gentle hug that I have you in my strong arms; that not even the power of death can snatch you away. I feel your frail little body, I can see your head sliding towards my left breast, prompting me to prop it up with my right hand, while looking at your gorgeous little face, especially your broad forehead, a landmark family feature. I try, albeit desperately to make you feel as safe and as comfortable as best as I can whilst you sit on my chest., I quietly wish, and hope that all the prognoses from the doctors will all turn out to be wrong! That somehow, your mother and I will be told that it's ok, and we can take you home.

As the nurse checks your breathing and informs me that you are really struggling to breathe now, I shed a tear or two; but I quickly look aside for fear that both your mum and the nurse will notice that I have been crying. I must be strong. Yes, strong for you, for your mum and your brothers. I must be a man, if only I know what that means. I guess the nurse must have realised that I am at breaking point. She asks us if we would like some photos taken: that is, of me and my little boy. I accept and she takes some pictures with the hospital camera and my mobile phone. Shortly after that you, Davi-Jayce, our beautiful butterfly, flap your wings and fly off from this miserable world to the place of bliss where you truly belong. At 12:40 p.m. you stop breathing, exactly 1 hour 20 minutes after you were born. Though I had been preparing my mind for this, the pronouncement by the nurse that you have left us feels like a hard kick in the balls. Yes, you heard me right, it feels like someone has kicked my manhood with all the strength they could muscle-up. It hurts badly. I feel like shouting, screaming out and saying no, it can't be! I feel confused, I cry, but I cannot let loose. I have to be strong, though I am screaming inside.

Losing you was not just the end of a life; it is the end of a dream, a future cut short. D-J, you are with us, you will always be a cherished, beloved son to your mother and me and to your brothers, until we meet again.

Delivering the placenta turns out to be the most difficult part. I have to ask for gas and air because I can't bear the pain. Upon every push, I feel like the placenta is out. Each push, though, only brings out lumps of blood. I am scared of being taken to theatre, so I push several more times until I can't push anymore; I have become very weak and I'm vomiting, as well.

The doctor is called to come and have a look. He tries to manually pull out the placenta but only the remaining cord comes out. I have already lost too much blood and the decision is taken for me to be rushed into theatre for the manual evacuation of the remains of the products of conception. I sign the consent form and I'm immediately rushed into theatre.

After several hours, under GA, (General Anaesthesia), I regain consciousness and the first thing I want to know is where Ankini and Lesra are and if they have had dinner. I become heavily anaemic with blood levels at 6.6. A blood transfusion is done the same day. It is not enough, however, and plans are made for further transfusions.

Meanwhile, baby is well wrapped and put on his cuddle cot and placed beside me. Twice, I think to myself that the baby is going to wake up due to the bleeping sounds from the machines in the recovery room and he and I will not have enough sleep. Twice, I remember that baby is never going to wake up from his deep sleep. At some point, I just place my hand over him and drift off to sleep.

It is 13 September 2017; I am so exhausted and need some rest. I have a funny type of headache which is affecting my sight, making it impossible for me to look at the lights. I switch off my phone, draw the curtains and grope for my bed in complete darkness so as to have a proper sleep. In my sleep, I had two incomprehensible dreams, the interpretations of which I'm yet to find out. Here's the first:

I am still dressed in the same little black dress I had on the day my waters broke; but I'm still pregnant and hooked up to a drip stand. I wheel the stand out and drive myself to a party where I meet most of the people I usually meet at parties. I find myself seated next to Anita and other Reading people (Friends). Lenin (Giddeon's friend) passes by and does not say a word to me. Giddeon comes in and just passes as though he has not seen me. I become furious and ask him where the boys are now that he is at the party. I grow worried that no one bothers to answer my question.

Then all of a sudden, a small bird lands on my shoulder and tells me that the reason no one can see or hear me is because I also died while I was giving birth to my baby. So, I ask the bird to tell everyone I am present. However, no one believes it when it does. Instead, they all send it out of the room, wondering what a bird is doing inside a hall.

Suddenly, I find myself back in my hospital bed. The same little bird flaps open very big wings, shields me with them and says: 'Sometimes in life, all you need is a hug.' Then I open my eyes and realise it is all a dream.

I am still wondering what this dream means. In another thought, I think this was Davi finally saying goodbye to me and he came in the form of a little bird with big wings. In my other dream,

I am giving lectures to some women working on their farms in the village. I am with the same little bird trying to talk to some women on their farm, but they keep throwing mud at us saying there is nothing I can offer them. I then ask who they think their daughters would want to be like. None of them will say they want to be like their moms when they grow up since all they see in their mothers is cleaning, washing, cooking, bearing children and working hard on the farms. I tell them that there is more to life than just working on the farms, washing, cleaning and ironing. I let them know there are ways of educating themselves, even without going into the classroom and having jobs. They ask how that's possible. So, I tell them they can have computers, enrol for online courses and work from home. They eventually drop their hoes and listen to what I have to say.

I hope this enlightenment is more than just another dream!

Interlude

Just before you move over to the next chapter, let me give you a brief summary of the relationship I have had with my babies from birth.

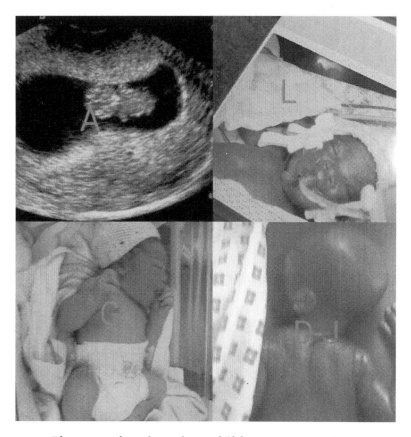

Photographs of my four children, representing
the relationship between them that I hold so precious
to my heart.

It is just so amazing to discover that sometimes we grieve so much on what we do not have and then forget to appreciate what we have at hand.

I've come to realise that no one baby's love can ever replace the other, whether in life or in death because each baby is unique. Angel, I miscarried her at just 8 weeks in 2005. The joys, the excitement knowing that I was pregnant for the first time, the anticipations, the plans, baby names, baby clothes etc. All these dreams and hopes and aspirations all shattered just at 8 weeks. I never met her, but I've always had a feeling she was a girl. She was never felt or touched or seen. I never grieved, I had no one to talk to.

Usually, it feels impossible to ever fully recover especially, emotionally from the pain and grief of losing a baby, however, falling pregnant again to me felt like a miracle. It was indeed a time of great joy, reflection, healing, and mixed emotions not only for myself but for the entire family. All my pregnancies after the first one were all emotionally complex pregnancies accompanied by feelings of anxiety, grief and guilt along with relief, excitement and elation. I counted each day as it came and passed until at 24+5days, Lesra popped out as if it was his right time. My world shattered again, but this time, I was ready to face the bull by the horn. I had cried and prayed for God to reverse the situation, but I guess it was already too late. I never had the chance to hold and cuddle him immediately after birth because he had to be taken for resuscitation. Same as Angel, I had never experienced how it felt like holding and cuddling a baby just from birth.

Then Came Gicles at 40+ 5 days—what a miracle. I was overwhelmed with a joy which changed and became the shedding of tears for having had such a big, almost 4 kg baby after previous experiences of miscarriage and the birth of a 980g baby. Unfortunately, I didn't really enjoy those first baby moments with him.

Finally Came D-J. Even though his life was short-lived, I spent most of the first baby moment time with him, which I never had the opportunity to do so before. Before he was born, I was ready to receive him and to say goodbye as well. I cuddled him skin to skin. I took as many photos with him as I could and then said goodbye. It was after D-J that I learned Lesra is a rainbow Baby. (A rainbow baby is a name coined for a healthy baby born after losing a baby due to miscarriage, infant loss, stillbirth, or neonatal death. It comes from the idea of a rainbow appearing in the sky after a storm, or after a dark and turbulent time). (https://www.healthline.com/health/pregnancy/rainbow-baby#The-symbolism-of-a-rainbow).

So you see, it's not how long someone lived on earth that determines the love that you give or show them. It's not how long they live that we have to decide whether to treasure them or accept them. Whenever you have the chance to tell or show someone you love them, do so because every little life matters, in the blink of an eye, that life can be taken away from you.

Chapter Three
Stages of Grief; Coping with Grief

When Davi-Jayce passed away, Ankini was very supportive, Even though he was heartbroken, he still said he had plans to do lots of things with his little brother; plans to play Lego together, plans to teach him about autism, and how to take care of their big brother Lesra. But all these plans were shattered within 1 hour and 20 minutes of D-J's very short life on earth.

Here below, is a conversation between my then 7-year-old and me not long after my loss. At this point, I had to run upstairs to cry. Isn't it amazing how far children's imaginations stretch? I realised how shaky my faith had been since the pain of losing my baby gripped me. Sometimes, all we need is the faith of children to snap out of these tragedies, but this is not easy because we aren't children. Through it all, I am still grateful for the gift of life: my life and the little life that was given to my son and the time I spent with him before he passed on. In every situation, always look at the happy side of things and be grateful. There always is that happy side of things if we decide to find it, if we try to look for ways to turn our sadness into gladness or obstacles into opportunities.

Ankini: Mum, what is the best gift that you want for Christmas?

Me: Don't worry. What I want for Christmas, no one can give me. (*walked into the kitchen to avoid the conversation. Ankini followed me.*)

Ankini: I know what you want.

Me: Tell me then

Ankini: You want Davi-Jayce back, right?

Me: But that's not possible, is it? (*fighting tears*)

Ankini: Yes, it's possible. How did God bring back Jesus from death? He can bring back Davi-Jayce if only you ask him.

Replaying this conversation makes me sort of giggle now. It's not because of the absence of the pain of loss; it's rather the acceptance of all that has happened that leaves my cheeks dimpled. Back then, I had to run upstairs to cry at that exchange. In order words, I had been helpless and could barely hide my tears from my little man. When grief strikes, we don't just snap out of it like that. We move from one stage of grief to another.

The information we can handle varies from one stage to another. It took the physical loss of D-J for me to understand that I had been grieving for more than 12 years.

I remember visiting Pat (my 73-year-old friend) in Hayling Island. After a lengthy discussion with her, she looked at me and said to me, 'Oh, Claris, you never had the time to grieve when you had Lesra'.

I told her that Lesra did not die so how could I have grieved him. Pat pointed out that grief does not have to be experienced with the physical loss of a baby or a loved one. She also mentioned that having Lesra premature and him growing up with disabilities are enough reasons for me to be grieving even without knowing.

When one has a child premature or with a disability, one grieves the child they could have had at full term. The remaining 3.5 months I was still going to be pregnant, all the plans, dreams and aspirations were all gone. The unfortunate thing, in this case, is, I never allowed myself to go through the emotions which accompany grief. I guess because life was so busy with the baby in the hospital, frequent hospital appointments, work etc.

Having a child with a disability or long term illness is also a reason to grieve. Unfortunately, I never knew I had to grieve a child that is very much alive. The reason why most will go through the stages of grief are that, no one expects to have a child with a disability, no one signs up for it. It strikes often when least expected. But when this happens, it is necessary to give yourself time to understand why you are feeling the way you are feeling, and also to be able to understand the situation. It is often said that there is no right or wrong way to grieve but there is a healthy and unhealthy way to grieve. I unconsciously grieved the child I would have had at full term and also the one I could have had without a disability. All my dreams, hopes and aspirations were gone.

When I look back, I remember I was constantly sad, angry and tearful most of the time and with little or no sleep and a massive loss of self-confidence or self-worth, little did I know that this was suppressed grief manifesting itself in different ways.

Dr Elisabeth Kübler-Ross' book 'On Death and Dying, the Five Stages of Loss and grief (Denial, Anger, Bargaining, Depression, and Acceptance), helped me gain an understanding and insight into the emotional and social experience of the death of my baby, and a greater understanding of all the emotions I was experiencing. At some point, I was wondering if I was really ok. I could not understand why I was experiencing all the different emotions. After I started reading On Death and Dying, I started having a better understanding of what I was going through, which greatly helped me in managing the emotions.

1. Denial: Even though denial is often regarded as negative, this is normally the first stage which helps one navigate through the other stages. Denial can be regarded as a coping mechanism in the short run. Initially, I never knew I was ever going to be happy again or even be able to face the rest of the world. At this stage, I refused to admit the reality that I was no longer pregnant and that my baby had actually died.

Although I had held and watched him take his last breath, prepared for his funeral and saw him buried, I refused to talk about D-J in the past tense especially as his due date was still approaching on 13 January 2018. I deliberately refused to talk about him in the past tense, given that, his due date was still in the future. So, I would always say, my baby was born in September 2017, but his due date is on 13 January 2018. I could at least console myself that I had a concrete reason not to say that my baby was supposed to be born.

How often I visited D-J was an indication that I was still in denial. I always told myself that his resting place was my second home where I had to go visit every day. Whenever I did not visit, I would be filled with guilt until the next time I went to visit him.

I thought not visiting often would mean that I had abandoned him. So, frequent visits were made with flowers daily or weekly. It may sound surprising, but denial and shock actually played a huge part in helping me cope and survive my grief journey. I went through a state of sudden, upsetting and unexpected experiences comprising of an acute medical condition which led to fluctuating levels of BP (Blood Pressure) and eventually led to heavy blood loss after delivery. My waters breaking and my baby's sudden arrival took my entire family by surprise.

How long shock lasts during grief varies from one individual to another as we don't have the same levels of resilience. I was upset and in disbelief, especially because it involved the suffering and the eventual death of my little baby boy. I was in a state of bewilderment. My mind was not clear about whether in reality, I was no longer pregnant.

At some point, I thought I was going insane. Being confused limits one's level of concentration. I considered this loss a major loss, as I had never experienced such in my life before and it had a huge effect on my capacity to think, feel and my ability to participate in daily life activities.

I realised I used to make several trips around the house looking for something which I would still forget. In most cases, I eventually would have to retrace my steps to be able to remember where I was going and what I was looking for. This also affected the way I communicated with my boys. I would say one thing while I meant the other. There were words like *read* instead of *eat*, *television* instead of *remote control*. Sometimes Ankini would remind me or simply ask if that was what I really wanted to say. Lesra would simply just stare at me when I was saying one thing but pointing at another. Even in my kitchen, I became a complete stranger. This affected me right up to the extent that on D-J's due date, I got so busy with the preparation of the thanksgiving mass we had offered on that day that I forgot Ankini had to go for his doctrine lessons. That was sad. Driving became a nightmare for fear of what might happen to me on the way.

2. Anger: I always thought I could be in control of so many things that could happen to me. Anger is a strong feeling of annoyance, displeasure and maybe hostility. When we are unable to control what happens to us or what has happened to us, we tend to get angry and frustrated. Anger is one of the most confusing emotions during the grieving process. It is very difficult for outsiders to fully understand one's anger during such a period. But what I know certainly is the fact that my anger only went to show the extent to which my D-J was loved and was an expression of how much I wanted him to stay. I think it was mostly at this stage I felt judged a lot.

Generally, it is difficult for someone to fully understand a situation until they have experienced it. Many did not understand what I was going through just because I wanted to save that little boy. Do you know what it means to go around for 4 days with a baby's leg hanging out in between your legs?

At some point, I became so frustrated and helpless, not knowing what I would do when I delivered our baby. I would have to watch him eventually die. I want to believe the anger during this period might also have resulted from a build-up of past happenings which the baby's death only came to intensify. Maybe things which could have been done and were not done most probably during pregnancy or sometime in the past.

It is unfortunate that if the anger at this stage continues for a long time without any help, it can lead to resentment. When faced with difficult circumstances like child loss, it may be a little easier to deal with the situation if there are no external factors to contend with. Dealing with people often makes it difficult when grieving or when hit by child loss. I was not only shocked by the unexpected arrival and death of my little baby, I was baffled by the treatment I received from some people around me. I knew I had gone through the normal stages which a woman would go through to have a baby–the labour pain and the painful delivery–and having to watch my baby pass away in the arms of his dad. To me, this was a baby like any other. I did not expect the rest of the world to have a different way of perceiving this. A baby should be regarded as a baby even if they don't live long after delivery.

These are some of the situations where expectations fail us. I had expected everyone to treat this little baby as any other baby but that was not the case and my expectations were not met.

At first, I could not understand why most people were so lukewarm. However, I eventually understood that everyone thought it was just a miscarriage. This intensified my anger. I felt judged, blamed, isolated and abandoned. At the same time, people were rejoicing each time a new baby got born after mine and everyone acted as though the live baby meant everything to the world when mine meant nothing. I was angrier because I thought I'd found myself in a situation where I was completely helpless.

I had always known I was always going to protect my kids even in death, but Davi-Jayce proved me wrong. I became angry and agitated towards anyone who loosely said anything that was related to childbirth or child loss. When a woman gives birth, everyone rejoices; but when another woman loses her child, everyone pretends it never happened. A few call, to check on her when it happens, and others carefully ignore mentioning the baby's name as if s/he never existed. Everyone seems to expect the woman or the family to move on or carry on with life as if nothing ever happened. We live in a world where child loss, be it miscarriage, premature birth, at full term or shortly after birth still appears to be a taboo subject. It is still considered by many as a very emotional and sensitive topic to talk about because it brings about bad memories. Those affected are made to be silent, decide to be silent or are not even able to mention their babies' names because they are afraid of being judged or labelled this or that.

Child loss or premature birth that leads to disabilities or death are still seen as something to be ashamed of because the thought goes that there is obviously something wrong with you, be it medically or you're suffering from an ancestral curse or a punishment from God. These common beliefs leave the woman in a state of uncertainty, constantly asking herself if she has actually done something wrong or if she had offended anyone in the past. When this happens more than once, she may even start believing that something is definitely wrong somewhere and this may lead to her becoming ashamed of herself for not being able to bring forth 'normal or live children'.

Before giving birth to D-J prematurely, I had experienced a miscarriage. After experiencing preterm birth, the second time with Davi-Jayce, life lost its meaning. Nothing or anyone mattered anymore to me. I felt I had just hit rock bottom. My self-esteem all vanished within seconds. I used to walk with my head and shoulders held high; suddenly, everything changed. I could not hold my head high anymore. If I was out and about, I felt like the whole world was staring at me.

Statistics show that more than 20 per cent of pregnancies end in miscarriages. The fact that there is no or a rather minimal conversation around this topic makes the individual to start believing they are to blame. This leads to feelings of failure, shame, anger, guilt and even insecurity.

3. **Bargaining**: I remember when my waters had just broke, standing in the middle of that hospital ward, I was so shocked and did not know what to do. When it finally dawned on me that a bucket of water had not been poured on me, but it was my baby's amniotic fluid gradually gushing out, I pleaded to God to reverse the situation. I told him I was ready at that moment to do anything He asked of me. I also said that God should just grant the baby a few more days in my tummy and that I was ready to go down the Neonatal Intensive Care Unit (NICU) route once more.

I found myself literally making a deal with God. That was bargaining. It is at this stage that guilt also hits one so bad. I thought of Job's story in the bible and I knew that if I had not doubted this baby's existence, he would not have died.

I also thought that if I had left the house and gone straight to the hospital on that fateful 7 Sept 2017, all these things may not have happened in the first place. I wished that I had gone to the A&E immediately when I felt the trickle down my thighs.

So, while trying to bargain with God, at this stage, I kept wondering what I did or where I went wrong, reflecting on why I did not act more quickly, when I felt there was something wrong.

4. **Depression**: Dr Ross states that depression is a commonly accepted form of normal. Depression is almost always immediately associated with grief. It will be necessary to know that Depression can co-exist. Depression comprises of the emptiness, the loss of interest I started experiencing when I finally realised that my baby was no longer here. Life did not seem real at all anymore. Within me, there was no other loss as painful as the death of an innocent baby.

I lost interest in everything and almost everyone around me. I could not go out to special occasions; I could not even stand the sound of people talking. Everything was irritating. I used to wake up in the morning, help to prepare the boys for school, drop them off and then come back home, draw the curtains and just stay in the living room all day without any lights on.

I remember one of my friends calling me using a video call. Unfortunately, I had forgotten that the curtains were still shut. So, he asked me if I was ok. I told him I was ok, and he said to me, you wouldn't be sitting in darkness and looking so tired and exhausted if you were. It was at that point that I realised I needed help.

Even before losing the baby, I had been battling with depression without knowing, or maybe I was in denial. After I had my now 10-year-old in 2010, I was diagnosed with Post Natal Depression, which I declined medications for, but I did accept some professional help for counselling, which was arranged at my older son's school. My doctor had suggested prescribing medications, but I declined. So, maybe looking back, I will say that it had to take the physical loss of a baby for me to realise that I had been grieving for almost 12 years without knowing. I had no choice but to agree to be placed on antidepressants. I must say they do have side effects like weight gain, but they are gradually helping. The body pains I feel most of the time, the constant tiredness and mood swings are manageable now. Some days, I feel like I can conquer the world but other days, I just feel like rubbish or have a feeling of worthlessness. Most importantly, identify and managing the triggers have been a great success.

5. Kubler – Ross identified **Acceptance** as the last stage of grief. Here, I am at a point of calmness, adjustment and readjustment and everything seems to be back to normal. At this point in my life, I seem to have finally acknowledged the death of my baby and know that I will be ok. I know that my baby will never come back and I am able to accept that this is how I am going to live for the rest of my life.

Accepting or acknowledging a situation is not a weakness but an acceptance of what has happened and that there will be new ways of living and adjusting to the changes that the loss has brought.

It is worth noting that accepting does not mean everything will be completely perfect. I still have good and bad days; but I must say that the good days far outweigh the bad. I feel more positive with a broader perspective in life. One thing's for sure, there will always be pain and sadness, but I know that I am moving forward with my grief and not moving on with it as many loosely put it.

Coping with Grief
The Power of resilience:

Psychology Today describes it this way:

"Resilience is that ineffable quality that allows some people to be knocked down by life and come back stronger than ever. Rather than letting failure overcome them and drain their resolve, they find a way to rise from the ashes." *(https://positivepsychology.com/what-is-resilience/).*
Resilience is simply the ability and tendency to bounce back after when we face disappointment, defeat, loss and failure, but instead of wallowing or letting things keep us down, we get back up and continue on with our lives. It was due to resilience that I was able to bounce back from grief and below are some of the tips which helped me through the process.

At the beginning of almost all grief journeys, it sometimes feels like it is impossible to ever fully recover emotionally from the pain of losing one's baby. However, there are a few helpful things/activities which I did. I hope they may help someone cope during their grief period.

- The loss of a baby comes with a lot of emotional pain. So, while I was trying to process the reality of my loss, I realised I was also trying to survive emotional pain. Therefore, taking time to learn and understand our emotions after loss can help us heal better. Which is why **the stages of grief** have been well explained in this book.

- I found that **journaling my emotions**, feelings and events around me helped enormously. One thing you wouldn't like when grieving is to be judged, and I found that writing down my thoughts in a book, no matter how raw the pain was, helped enormously. It is due to the journaling that Grief to Grit came into existence.

- At some point, while grieving, it is expected that one may struggle with their mental health. If at any one point you think you are struggling, seek medical or professional help. I sought counselling and also I accepted to go on antidepressants. It may not apply to everyone, but it is necessary to know that an untreated mental health problem may lead to more complicated problems in the long run. Taking care of our health, both mental and physical, are of utmost importance.

- It is often said, sharing is caring, personally, sharing to the right person at the right time is even better. **Talking to individuals or joining support groups or joining an online community of like-minded** people with similar experiences helps enormously. In this milieu of individuals, you know someone will relate with your story, you know someone will understand. You are fully aware that you are in a safe space to speak out knowing that you will be heard and not be judged or stigmatised.

- Developing an attitude of gratitude is one of the greatest lessons I have learned during my grief journey. Many a time, we forget to appreciate what we have, we focus our attention, our energy on what we do not have right there in front of us. When I started focusing on the baby I had rather than the one I thought I was going to have, I felt relieved and more healing came along. I focused my attention more on the precious moments I had with him, the 120mins he had on earth and all the good things and the good people who supported me during the period.

- I also learned how to ask for practical help when I could not handle everything myself, which is what most often individuals do not feel comfortable doing. I do understand this since sometimes, they feel like they are being a burden on others.

- During moments of grief, one can have triggers in various forms; ranging from birthdays, anniversaries, mention of the baby's name, flowers and so on. This varies from one individual to another. I used to have flowers as gifts from friends who came to condole with us. The sight of flowers hurt. After I had a massive breakdown in a shop just at the sight of flowers, I decided that instead of allowing myself to breakdown in tears each time I'd spot flowers, I would instead take the flowers to decorate the baby's grave. So I made sure every month I went to the cemetery, all dressed and made up with a bouquet of flowers. This helped me both emotionally and physically since I was looking forward to leaving the house at least once a month. I found this quite therapeutic as journaling (mentioned above).

- There is a certain degree of self-neglect during grief. When depression sets in during grief, we tend to lose interest in activities we used to enjoy or even just having the urge to go out of the house is barely there. Some days I literally forgot to have a bath or even do my hair. Again, there is that aspect of grief, where guilt sets in. At the moment where I wanted to make myself happy, I started feeling guilty that I was moving forward a bit too fast with the grief. At some point, I learned that self-care is not a luxury but a necessity. It is absolutely important to take care of yourself always including when you are grieving a loved one.

- As a Christian, I realised that **prayers** deepened my faith, especially after I had lost faith in everyone, myself, including God. I needed to have a greater understanding of God's purpose in my life, and it was only through prayers that this happened. Even though God answers **prayers**, oftentimes, He answers them in ways we least expected. So, while grieving, do not underestimate the power of prayer.

- I naturally love music and singing. I also discovered that all through my pregnancy, I had developed a liking to a particular genre of Music. When I finally lost D-J, I discovered that each time I was feeling low or overwhelmed, I listened to music and felt better, especially listening to some of the songs I used to listen to while I was still at the hospital. Sometimes during grief, words fail us, music, therefore, creates a legitimate space to **grieve**, which allows us to connect and feel with others.

Chapter Four
Supporting a Bereaved Individual Through Grief

Have you ever imagined travelling without direction? Grieving the loss of a loved one is like travelling around the world in just a few days without any idea of the direction you are taking. At some point, you feel like you are just moving in circles. Some people who used to be close to you gradually drift away because they don't know what to tell you. Some may simply not think your approach to grieving is appropriate or for some, your loss may have brought up memories of a loss they once had and which they had always wanted to avoid, due to the pain and the hurt that comes along with some losses. Well, no two individuals are the same as well as no two individuals grieve the same. Individuals' approaches to handling grief vary depending on many factors.

What matters most is understanding what works for the person in question. Time may heal all wounds, but not all scars. When one experiences any form of loss, there are friends, or family members who may really try to get to you so they can help or console you during this devastating moment, but they may ignorantly end up saying the wrong thing. You can't blame them. At least, they tried to help. They've never been through what you've been through. They can only try to imagine. That's the reason I decided to come up with this section to guide such well-meaning people.

I've recently found myself in situations that have left me in tears. I mean due to small things, things that wouldn't have meant a big deal to me before. I don't want to believe my reactions mean that I'm overly sensitive or easily offended. Because of recent events, I do take longer to carefully choose my words. I am slower to make judgements about situations. I'm more thoughtful about how my actions may affect someone. It's my hope that sharing my grief journey will raise awareness, help other grieving parents and help people learn how to morally support their loved ones who go through grief.

These are things well-meaning people might say and how they might be interpreted: Statements that can harm during grief.

⌘ Do not worry; God needed a new flower in his Garden. If this is the case, then God only decided to choose my own flower then.

⌘ God does not make mistakes in choosing his Angels.

⌘ God needed another Angel around his throne.

⌘ Only God knows why. I wish I knew what that 'why' was, and then maybe I would not be hurting so much.

⌘ Your baby is in a better place

⌘ God does not give you what you cannot carry.

⌘ Only water poured, thank God the calabash did not get broken. What if you say this to a woman who has been battling fertility issues for years and this was her last chance? What if you say this to someone who has had several miscarriages, and this was the last time before she hits menopause? Just imagine what she will be going through after hearing that statement from someone.

⌘ You have to be grateful that you already have other children. It is good to know that no child can replace another even in death.

⌘ Thank God you are still young; God will give you more children. It is hard to know if, after the devastating child loss, she will still be able to have another ever again.

⌘ You have to get over it and move on! I am wondering: does one get over unconditional love? Do you move on from a loved one?

⌘ So sorry, but it happens to so many other women out there. So, you are not the only one. Will this statement help or make you feel any better?

⌘ I had an unborn child just like you. If you are not sure what she had, please ask.

⌘ On a daily basis, people have different categories of problems they face, so do not act as if you are the only one.

⌘ Things are better this way because you do not know what the child would have turned out to be.

⌘ Maybe if the child survived, you would have been having two children with disabilities.

⌘ Let me know if you need anything

Some of these statements could be very hurtful depending on who makes them and their relationship with the grieving person. Take, for instance, this statement: 'on a daily basis, people have different categories of problems they face, so do not act as if you are the only one.' Such a statement could be easily waved aside if it's coming from a total stranger. From a close friend or relative whom you expect to understand you better, it could be shocking and hurt beyond words.

Whenever a family is hit by a tragedy, everyone is affected in various ways and different degrees. However, the woman usually feels worse, especially in cases where she almost lost her life as well as the life of her baby. After the event, she may become traumatised and that may go on for a very long time if proper help is not sought. I still don't understand why no one ever admonishes women for loving their children too much but people find it very easy to criticise them for grieving too much. As women, we love deep; so, we grieve deep. So, if a statement like this is to be made, it should obviously not be to someone who almost lost her life in childbirth, who was at the point of sacrificing her own life for her child to live.

When I was asked to terminate D-J, I refused because I wanted him to live despite all the odds. I knew there were risks of infection, heavy blood loss and maybe both of us dying or long term disabilities if he survived. Unfortunately, his life wasn't saved, but mine was. Yes, I may not be the only one going through difficult times; I may not be the only woman who has suffered child loss. I am not the only woman who has had four pregnancies in her life with two surviving children; but I am the one who endured the physical, emotional and psychological trauma. So, please let us be careful with the words we use because they may reopen an old wound that someone is trying to heal.

The truth about the statements above is that they may or may not be hurtful to all. Usually, this depends on what context the statement is made in and how it is perceived. However, here are a few tips on how or what can be said to a grieving parent.

Some Statements That Heal

⌘ This child was unique, special and irreplaceable. I know children are not interchangeable and the fact that you can have other children does not lessen the grief of losing this one.

⌘ Tell me more about your pregnancy and your baby...I'm interested and I'm not tired of hearing the same stories. I know sometimes you need to keep going over those events until they seem real and more tolerable.

⌘ How are you doing today? If you don't feel like answering the phone, I'll just leave a message to let you know that I love you and was thinking about you. I'm sure you'll return my call when you feel up to it.

⌘ Do not worry, God will one day heal your broken heart and will probably fill the hole that this tragedy has created

⌘ The simplest one to say is just, I am sorry for your loss

⌘ Tell me what happened

⌘ Are you ok to talk about the baby?

⌘ I would like to hear you talk about your baby: how old is s/he? What's his favourite toy; his/her name?

Some practical tips to help a grieving family

Apart from the healing words mentioned above, here are some practical ideas to support an individual or family following the devastating loss of a loved one/baby.

➢ **Call to check how they are doing.** When I was still at the hospital, I recall quite a few people/friends would call to check how I was doing. This was so much appreciated. Just a simple conversation with someone could go a long way to help the person's healing process.

I remember the whole Luton family. The pain I saw on Sister Imma's (Lesra's God Mother) face told so many stories. If I could see tears rolling down her cheeks, then that alone explained the pain she felt and the memories which D-J's passing brought to her. The sadness on Justin's (Lesra's Godfather) face could not be hidden at all. Anita, Loretta, sister Bri (friends) and a few others would call me almost daily. However, there were still those who could not call because the situation was so sorrowful they had no idea what to say.

. **See the family as whole.** Most often, attention is paid more to the woman. However, it is a good idea to check on the entire family as well. One of my friends never spoke to me for several weeks after the baby had passed away. Given that she had had a similar experience in the past, she was perfectly aware of the situation. To her, it brought back so many sad memories and she felt more comfortable talking with my husband about the baby. That was perfectly fine by me. Helping my husband face the situation, I want to believe, was indirectly helping me, as well.

⌘ **Include their babies' names on cards.** I have reasons to believe many people don't know how important this is for the grieving family, yet. Because a child has died, it is considered that he/she is no longer part of the family and so the child's name should not really be mentioned anywhere or even remembered. This could be quite painful to the bereaved parents because they really crave to see their child's name being written somewhere or being remembered by family or friends. I always wished that someone could remember my baby's name, to talk about him or to write his name on a birthday card, Christmas or Easter card.

I do appreciate Lin who sent my family a Christmas card at the end of which she boldly added, and of course, Little Davi-Jayce, RIP. This melted my heart. I was so excited and so grateful that she remembered him. Of course, she did. She has had similar experiences of child loss before and she knowsexactly how it feels for one's child to be remembered, regardless of whether they are alive or dead. Mentioning the child's name helps with the parent's grief.

I also take into consideration that no two grief experiences are the same. Some parents may like to have their child's name remembered by many, while others would rather have it otherwise. Since there is a lot of emotions attached to child loss, there is that tendency of people not knowing whether to mention the child's name on the card or not.

⌘ **Ask and talk about their baby.** Most parents, especially the mums, feel good when they talk about their baby's name. This is because they want to keep the memories alive. I wished that someone else could mention D-J's name or even remember him. So, I urge everyone that in as much as the loss is huge, if you have the chance to ask about the baby's name, it will always be much appreciated by most parents.

⌘ **Offer to take them out:** Sometimes the grieving process can become so overwhelming the parents find it difficult continuing with normal life just after a child has passed away. If the parent has other children, please spare a few minutes to take those children out for a walk if you can. I am so grateful for Elaine who spared a few hours of some days to take Lesra out. Vincent, as well, played an important role by taking Ankini out whenever he could. Lesi (A good friend) visited and opted to take me out to Costa Coffee. Despite all the pain I was going through and the fact that baby was still at the funeral directors, I still had to gather the courage to go out and take some fresh air. I must say it was quite therapeutic

⌘   **Offer to do shopping:** If she is still at the hospital or even if she is already at home. Some periods of the year, especially festive seasons, birthdays and death dates come with a lot of triggers. They can be physically and mentally draining when a grieving person has to go shopping. Sometimes, just the thought of it scares one for the simple fact that your loss seems to have brought your world to a standstill and everyone else's life seems to be going on perfectly well. It is difficult to predict what may or may not trigger a breakdown. Usually, one becomes overly careful, trying not to go out. The thought of seeing someone pushing a baby pram with a baby inside could be inconceivably painful. The desire to avoid people and questions can also be what prevents the woman from going out.

On 23 December 2017, I went into Tesco to do Christmas shopping and all of a sudden, I realised I had been going around a particular aisle several times. Before I knew it, I broke down in tears beside the fresh flowers. I stood there with my trolley of groceries; tears uncontrollably streaming down my cheeks. In as much as I tried to fight and choke them back, the tears just flowed on. Then, I eventually decided to let them flow.

One lady passing by me asked if I was okay, I managed a nod in response. She made to leave but came back and gently took my hand and told me I couldn't be crying yet saying everything was fine. So, she held my hand and then gave me a hug, then apologised, saying she was just from the gym and a bit sweaty. After our encounter, I thanked her, I felt better and proceeded to checkout.

While there, the tears started again, and the cashier looked at me as if she wanted to ask if everything was fine. For some reason, she chose not to say anything but rather, she got a piece of paper and wrote, Ho Ho! Merry Christmas, everything will be fine. I forced a smile through my tears and thanked her as I left. This is probably why it would be a good idea if you could ask a friend if they can help you with the shopping. Do not decline help when it is being offered.

⌘   Please, just in case the woman has other children, take food to her other kids at home instead of opting to take food to the hospital. I can remember very kind and caring friends who prepared food for me while I was at the hospital. This was a very kind gesture and really thoughtful of them. However, when in hospital, one is being served hospital meals every day. So, I actually suggested to my friends that instead of them bringing me food to the hospital, it would be a good idea for them to take the prepared food to my kids at home. It was very much appreciated, since it saved my husband time and energy from cooking. I can still remember the spaghetti which Loretta (one of my friends) prepared and Lesra absolutely loved it, the stew and other dishes cooked by Sister Bri (Ankini's Godmother) which served the family for weeks while I was in hospital. I also remember the food which Miranda and Lillian (friends) prepared; it really helped for a number of days.

Chapter Five
Seeing the Grit in Grief

When tragedy strikes, lessons should be learned so that experiences will be used in the long run to help others. (C. Angafor)

Experience is what you gain when you did not get what you wanted. (Randy Pausch)

As you must know by now, I have been through so much pain from loss. Love though has been my strength through all this. The love of God, love for myself, and love for D-J whom I know wants me to be happy, love for my husband, love for my children, love for a better world when I'm no more, so much love. Nothing heals like love in all its dimensions. But the problem with love is it's impossible to genuinely love without getting hurt. The two go together, but one should not be confused for the other. Love is perfected imperfection; pain is failed love. You get the link, don't you? These two always have to fight and the stronger always carries the day.

Having gone through all what I went through, I decided to use my experience to connect with people who've had a similar experience and to help those who've not had a similar experience to be able to understand and connect with us.

By writing this book, I seek to raise awareness that every little life matters. Forget about time, we can't draw a line between giving birth and losing the baby after two hours or 20 years. The pain is just the same. The heart doesn't know a thing about time; it's the brain that knows everything about it. The heart only knows how to love and get hurt. Hence, child loss is loss irrespective of the gestation period. The whole world, therefore, deserves to know that my little boy existed and left a vacuum on his departure. I'm in no way appealing for self-pity. I just happen to have chosen to break the silence over pregnancy and infant loss because I believe that every experience lived, is worthy, valuable and has the power to transform lives. You'll not be wrong calling me the leading voice of hope and empowerment.

We, as a family, have always been an army despite other challenges. This tragedy came like a bomb that took us unawares, tearing us apart as everyone sought refuge in their own way. Love brought us back together though to fight against the common enemy. We won and we're stronger now. Our arsenal, I'm proud to say, is top-notch now. I can't pretend to you it doesn't hit us still, I mean the pain of it all, but when you have love as anaesthesia, you become numb to pain.

It wasn't until I celebrated D-J's life with friends that I started facing the rest of my life without him. He now and forever will be a cherished memory. You must have understood by now how tough the grief journey can be. Many have asked me:

'How do you do it? You have gone through a lot and are still able to smile at the end of the day.'

What they don't know is, that's what I let them see. I've gone past that initial phase of grief that was hard to control.

Death might be as old as the world itself, but still always takes us by surprise and leaves us grieving as though it were something new. We're hardly ever ready for it. The death of one's baby or death, in general, isn't something one sits and prepares their mind for, before it happens. We live in an era where most people would rather sneak up on your WhatsApp or Facebook status to find out what is happening to you, rather than actually call or write to you to find out how you are doing.

Grief can make those closest to you become further away when you need them the most. A time where you make friends and find love in friendships you never expected. Most often, when there is bereavement, people contribute money to support the bereaved family. This is really great, especially as it eases the financial burden on the grieving family. One thing that's certain though is that no amount of donated money will ever bring back the deceased. So, the place of moral support cannot be overemphasised. Giving someone a call, swinging by to check on them and leaving a message, are just a few of the very many ways to go about this.

Child loss should not be considered a taboo. People should not be stigmatised because it happened to them or because they find it hard to get over. In fact, one never gets over the loss of a loved one. One can move forward without necessarily getting over it. Let them grieve till they feel better rather than criticising them for exaggerating their pain. You're not in their heart, so you know not how they feel.

I want to talk about D-J because he lived. Some people go, oh, so he had a name. With an odd look on their face whenever I mention his name. Yes, he unapologetically did, and I unapologetically call him by that.

You are expected to shut up and be quiet because when it happened to others, they did just that. This was somebody I carried in my womb; I felt his kicks; then carried him in my arms and felt his heartbeat. I still have his imprints on my bare chest because that is where he laid before I handed him over to his dad until when he took his final breath. How in the world do you expect me to act as though he never existed?

If that's what it takes to be an actress, then I guess I'm happily poor at it. They say things like, 'it was just a tiny little baby you never knew, so don't weep.' How charming! I started talking with D-J from the very first day I confirmed he was inside me.

The babies who pass away, their names are hardly ever remembered on any Christmas or greetings card. I understand this may be quite sensitive. But tell me, which parents wouldn't be happy, even if this happiness moves them to tears, if they received a small card assuring them that their departed beloved is in heaven sending them kisses.

In as much as some may want to forget the memories of their babies, many others will want to keep and treasure these memories. Sometimes some people want to say something but don't know exactly what to say. This moral support is very important, believe me. If you can't say anything good, don't badmouth. Let's just treasure the little moments we have with our loved ones; let us show them how much they mean to us because, in less than the blink of an eye, we may never see them again. As D-J proved to us, life is too short. The good news is that it's not the length of the life that determines the beauty of it.

The Mirror Effect

When I went in to be checked and blood was discovered in my urine, I was sent to the assessment ward. It was then that I decided to call Lin (my manager then), just to let her know that I wasn't at the training. A few hours later, I was wheeled to Willows ward (a comfortable and quiet room set aside for parents who are about to lose their babies or who have lost their babies). I had to wait for my husband to come so they could discuss the options that were available. While waiting, I called and broke the devastating news to Lin. In her usual kindness, she came round with my handbag, which I had left on my desk. When she stepped through the door, she looked at me and all she said was, 'oh Claris, I'm so sorry.' She held my hands and gave me a hug. It was a friendly and motherly hug in one package, an unusually warm hug from a manager, especially given that she is a white British lady. I felt at home, which always had been the case with her. Only that this was different. She could understand what I was going through. She could feel my pain just by peering into my eyes. She didn't need an explanation.

When we all sat down, she wiped her tears and helped to clean mine off my face. Then she asked me what the doctors had said. I told her and she asked if I was going to be taken to the theatre for the termination. She assumed that was what I had chosen. When I said no, she was shocked and all she could say was, 'Claris, you're a brave woman.' She still held my hands and, once more, she told me she was so sorry.

Going back a few months prior to that when I discovered I was pregnant at about 10 weeks, I decided to tell her, as my manager and as a mother. The day I decided to break the news to her, I kept thinking of what approach to take and how to start saying it. I never knew what her reaction would be—what she would say or do. That fateful morning,

I calmly walked from my desk over to hers and quietly told her while seated.

'Lin I've got something to tell you and please I hope you won't judge me.'

'Ok, Claris! I'm listening.'

'I'm about 10 weeks pregnant and please don't judge me on this. I know I just turned forty, it wasn't planned, but I'm keeping the baby.'

Her reaction was unexpectedly amazing and really sweet. Immediately after I finished talking, she stood up, held me and hugged me so tight. She had this bright and beautiful smile and excitement on her face, similar to that which would be seen on a mother who has been waiting for her daughter for ages to make this important announcement. Her reaction did not only surprise me, it allayed my fears.

Then she spoke:

'Claris, yes I know you're 40. Yes, you didn't plan for the baby, but that's no reason for me to judge you or anyone. I know you've had difficulties in the past with childbirth, but every child is different. What matters is how you feel and how ready you are.'

Then she went on to ask if Giddeon was already aware. I told her yes and she asked if he was ok with it. It was still a yes.

'So now, all you have to do is start looking after yourself and baby. Make sure you have the right care from the doctors and just relax and enjoy your pregnancy.'

Then she asked if I would like her to tell the rest of the team. Not yet, I responded. Our agreement was sealed.

Going back to when she met me in Willows ward with my hands in hers, tears in her eyes, I felt her pain. Lin could easily connect with me because she had also lost her baby who would have been 40 years. Yes, my age, mate. Almost one year earlier, Lin's daughter lost her baby at 5 months and it was only 5 months since Lin's sister got snatched by the cruel hands of cancer. And there was I, her staff member sitting right there about to lose a baby. So, Lin struggled with the memories of her son, who would have been 40, her daughter's baby, the pain and sorrow her daughter went through and the loss of her sister.

It was a devastating moment for her as well given her past experiences with child loss. But she was strong for me at that moment, for which I was and still am grateful. The twist of the whole baby Davi-Jayce's story was that I was secretly planning that Lin was going to be Davi-Jayce's Godmother. Alas, that didn't happen. God's ways are not ours.

Now, you probably must be wondering what the mirror effect has to do with all this. Do me a favour and forget about any mirror effect you may have known up to now, just for this part of this book, at least. I found a lot of peace when Lin hugged and sympathised with me. Lin was like a mirror through which I could see myself and my predicaments. I could connect with her. I felt better around her, knowing that she'd been through a similar ordeal. She, as well, could see herself in me. I reflected her broken past. We both sent out vibrations, we both were so familiar with this and it naturally drew us together. Now, that's what I call the healings of the mirror effect.

It's been a bitter-sweet journey. Sometimes, it still feels and hurts like yesterday, but I'm so grateful and happy for the more beautiful, more purposeful, more determined and more intentional person I've become over these months.

Someone said I could have handled it better because I've been down a similar route before. No two journeys can be the same. At least, I never ran away or avoided the situation. I stayed in there and I pulled through. Experiencing tragedies several times in life does not necessarily mean you are capable of handling them better than before. Each experience comes with a new lesson to be learned and a new you to be born.

I can proudly say now again, that when God puts one in a situation, he does not abandon us there, he gives us a road map and guides us all the way. He helps us handle what we have been given.

A second encounter may also be an opportunity to better understand God's purpose in our lives. It may equally be a chance for us to seek His face better and ask Him what he wants us to do with these experiences

We all know that when struck by any form of tragedies, it is human to be in shock, in denial, in anger, in shame or even feeling depressed before we get to the acceptance stage. Sometimes these emotions may blind us from seeing and acknowledging or even understanding the message God is passing across to us.

It is absolutely necessary to take time to feel, understand and acknowledge these emotions. It is also important to recognise that if your tragedy was the loss of a loved one, then the bereaved do not need to forget and leave the deceased behind but can integrate them into their future lives by means of a continuing bond. They can actually move forward without moving on. Even though people usually loosely say, you have to move on and forget. Really?

Regardless of which approach people take in handling tragedy, the most important part of supporting the person lies in being with them, listening intently to their story, acknowledging their feelings and guiding them to work towards a new, different and meaningful life without the deceased, and not being judgmental or avoiding the person.

Making Miracle from Misery

Sometimes we don't choose our journeys but when we find ourselves in one, God gives us the travel map to go through. The journey will be a smooth or a rough one depending on how well we make use of the travel map that was given to us.

My journey might have been a rough ride, but it's been amazing in its own special ways. Hardly could I ever have thought myself capable of someday getting used to it, but you know what time does to pain and everything else. Seeing the beautiful hands of God in everything is the best therapy ever. It could be very tough, but it's a muscle we should all train, whatever we conceive Him to be. Like I said, God is acceptance, perseverance, love, strength, courage and more.

I remember when I just got hit by this tragedy, I would cry most of the time because I thought he could have been saved but wasn't. However, it was important to cry while seeking God's face. Crying made me feel better, God made me feel great; I needed both. At first, it was tears of denial, then tears of acceptance, when God stepped into the picture, it became tears of love for an Angel I strongly believe is enjoying his time with other Angels. Dealing with this has been a whole process which is still ongoing; but it's been all about dealing with it and not denying it. Tears may all take a liquid form, but not every drop of tear we see translates into grief.

I had always known I was at risk of having preterm babies and, in my subconscious, I was always ready to walk the Neonatal Intensive Care Unit (NICU) journey. What I was never ready for was my baby coming early and not being able to be saved even though he wanted to live. So, it was just natural that I got hit. As a matter of fact, I still would've been hit hard had I known beforehand that D-J was going to end up like that. It's a bad thing to suppress grief.

But now, when I walk down memory lane, I no longer cry, not because I don't feel hurt and I'm not angry, rather because I can now crack a genuine smile. I have given myself the chance to seek the help that I need and also to work on my mindset. I have learned that no matter how sad a situation is, I could always look at the bigger picture and ask myself what is it that I can learn from the experience so that I can use my experience to help others who are in similar situations. If there is one major thing I have learnt during this journey, it's the power of gratitude. I have learned to appreciate even the very little things in life. When I look back, I have actually realised that sometimes we fail to acknowledge what we have had just because we expected something else.

Some never got to see their babies, others never knew their baby's sex, some never had the chance to hold their babies, others never felt their baby's heartbeat, movement etc. But all these, I did. But the sense of loss was still just as bitter. I feel grateful for the 80 minutes of communion with my D-J, but I felt lost without him and found the definition of love in him: love is mute; love lets go if it's the right thing to do without loving any less. So, I love and hate him at the same time without loving him any less.

During or after tragedies, human beings either become stronger or weaker; they either fall or rise; they're either broken or mended. Whichever happens, it's our decision and our responsibility to be happy again. No two humans are the same, which means reactions to tragedies naturally differ from one person to another. As for me, I have made a conscious and deliberate determined effort to transform my tragedy into something meaningful. One thing I kept asking God was for Him to show me the meaning of all the experiences I have had, to open my eyes wider and let me be able to see the purpose in all I have been through. At some point, I discovered, it needed a mindset shift. I had to learn and to start believing in the fact that tragedies do not come into our lives to destroy us but to give us another beautiful meaning to life. Barack Obama once said that, 'Crises do not come into our lives to destroy us, but they have a way of sharpening our focus.'

D-J's 80 minutes on earth were a turning point in my life. After grieving for a long time, I was inspired. I learned to channel this energy into doing something that will make the world a better place, no matter how small it may be. These 80 minutes gave me the password to a creative box that was lying idle in me.

When I was off work, I realised that each time I was really low, I played Candy Crush. Then I started thinking of what I could do to keep myself busy in a positive way and be able to help others out there, especially those who have been down this lane before. So, I discovered a group of ladies who meet every Tuesday just to chat, have a cup of tea and a cake and in the process, they teach others how to create beautiful designs with beads. I eventually learned how to create beautiful beaded bracelets, necklaces and watches and other items which I used to donate to women who have lost a baby, as a memory. The watches I created acted as a constant reminder to me and everyone else that life can just be as short as 80 minutes. I can confidently say that everything works together for good. My tragedy has now become my joy. The bracelets, necklaces, watches and related items are made for grieving parents with the aim of them wearing smiles on their faces despite what they may be going through. When life knocks you down, try to look up because if you can look up, then you can get up. (Les Brown).

In addition to my new grief-relief craft, I also created an Every Little Life Matters campaign with the aim of raising awareness.

I believe that more can and should be done to save infants from dying. I couldn't just have agreed to terminate my D-J's life just because that was the last option THEY said was left. The world can and should be better. I chose conservative management despite seeing death dangle before my very eyes. I could still feel him move; I could still feel his kicks. How was I supposed to take my own baby's life away and live happily with it? A true mother's heart isn't designed that way. How could I have denied life from a little being that had been living within me that long? I had already come to terms with the fact that he could not be resuscitated (though I secretly nursed hopes of someday laughing with him). I wanted D-J alive and was given the chance. I thank God for that.

On October 13th 2017, I started a campaign called, 'Every Little Life Matters.' so that the voices of countless families could be heard. Families who wished their voices to be heard to the moment they felt something was wrong; families of all the babies who are not given the chance to live because they are too small to be resuscitated.

Let's join the 'Every Little Life Matters' campaign, be it for just a minute. It's worth it, believe me. Before I had my baby,

I cried, I mourned, and I wept. I was ready to welcome him and at the same time, say goodbye. My Baby lived for 1 hour 20 minutes; every little minute spent with him was worth it.

Though I still forced myself to cling to hope against the doctors' words, I painfully realised that the pregnancy was the only time I had to be with him because there was no guarantee I could have him alive. I learned to cherish every little movement he made, especially given that his foot was already out, every hiccup, every kick, the way he felt in my womb, the mere fact that he was in me, etc. Everything seemed to be some sort of communion. He used to be described by the sonographer as chubby jaws, a very happy little baby. All I know is he liked to play and enjoyed music a lot. Because He lived, He mattered.

I remember every time I went for check-ups, I would get comments like, oh, what an active little man he is, with chubby jaws. D-J was not shy, showing everyone that he was a boy but was shy showing us his face. Now, D-J lives and basks in the eternal love of the highest God. The newest and the most handsome Angel in Heaven and I await the day I will be reunited with him to share that love and to share the bond we both had.

What a difference just two weeks in the womb can make to a little baby. I imagine what a massive difference two weeks could have made to Davi-Jayce. My waters had gone when I was 21+5 weeks. It is usually believed that when the waters have broken, especially at this early stage of gestation, the baby cannot survive because there is no more amniotic fluid to help the baby's lungs, etc. But my little fighter fought through all the odds and stayed in there for another 4 days just to have me hold and cuddle him.

During all this, I begged, wished, hoped and prayed for him to stay in there just for 2 more weeks. I was completely ready to go through that journey which I had once gone through with Lesra. I was ready to risk everything, even my own life, just for my baby to live. I was ready against all odds, but God sure had other plans.

The hole remains unfilled in my heart and soul, the pain still bites, a bite I can't pinpoint. But the more I learn to accept the pain, the broader my smile and the radiance on my face.

Although his coming into my life was not planned, I cherished and treasured every moment I had with him gradually growing in me. Though I shed tears when I discovered his existence, I did because I was scared; I thought I was not prepared. I feared because I thought with my past experiences with previous pregnancies, I was not going to cope. In all, it did not really matter how prepared I was before having my baby, but how happy and ready I was to welcome the baby. It's hard to ever be financially prepared enough; but I was psychologically, mentally and emotionally ready. Davi-Jayce's passing away has made me reflect a lot.

A Chance to Live

I see life here on earth as nothing but an amazing illusion. Nothing here is real, not even our lives, but the illusion must go on. I once asked myself the difference between someone who lives for a minute and another who lives for 200 years. Believe me when I say I would be lying if I claimed to have found or think I will ever find an answer to that. There are three things here: we are born, we live, and we die. Any other thing else is just the details of one of these three. Once we have been conceived, life is worth living, regardless of how long or how short it may be. I'm more than grateful D-J got to be born, lived and died. It was 80 minutes of love and tenderness.

Love, happiness, loss, pain and anger...Humans only alternate from one of these feelings to another. Don't mix the joy of the love and the pain of the loss. They could be two sides of the same coin, but they're different even when they complement each other.

Memories can either be good or bad, but the most painful ones are those you take home in a box after losing your baby to extreme premature birth.

D-J's short life on earth reminds us of the illusion of a tomorrow. What we actually call tomorrow is just another part of today. What if our lives were to go on for just one long day without any darkness to distinguish between day and night? Would there still be a tomorrow? Considering it were, would the conception still be the same? I may be sad, but I'm the proud mum of a Handsome Angel in Heaven, sitting at the right hand of God.

Yes, it's time to speak out. Let's give our little ones the chance to live even if it's just for a minute. If your little one was too young to be resuscitated, were you given the chance to have them alive, would you? Every little life matters, be it just for a minute or two. My little angel fought to stay alive. Unfortunately, he came too early, too soon and had to go too soon, but he lived before leaving.

D-J taught me to be strong. Believe me when I say what I have now is a far better version of the person I used to be.

That notwithstanding, I am still human. There are times that I still ask questions:

- Where did I go wrong?
- What did I do that was not right?
- When did everything start going bad?
- Who did I offend?
- Was there something I could have done that I did not do?
- Did the doctors and midwives give their best?
- Did they miss anything?
- Is there anything they could have done to prevent this?
- Is there anything that can be done to save others future from such pain?
- Is there anything anyone could have done?
- Is there really a future?

Asking questions makes me feel better in the short run, but what happens in the long run as these questions may not have answers or complete ones?

Asking such questions can feel like torturing oneself. It may send me into a guilt trip. Asking questions can leave me feeling empty. It may leave me with little confidence in myself. Such questions can make me resentful. There can be a tendency to feel that those around could have done something to help. This feeling alone could leave me very hateful and full of anger with those closest, especially if they were not caring or supportive enough during the pregnancy.

Asking questions may hurt, but it could be therapeutic, as well. Asking relevant questions could push our understanding further and put us in a better position to help ourselves and/or others in similar circumstances. It is reflecting on what could have or couldn't have been done. Questions could enrich you and make you more knowledgeable, more confident, and lead to a sense of belonging and a sense of purpose. This happens especially when the right questions are asked, and the right answers are sought.

One of the ways to cope with grief is to reach out to those who have had similar experiences and who can understand. I reached out to some of my friends, some were not too comfortable sharing. At the same time, others did not hesitate to share and give their voice to the experience of child loss to inspire others and also to seek healing.

Experiences of Friends

Guardian Angel

I have had a rocky relationship with pregnancies. Let's just recap this in a sentence: I've been pregnant 6 times but have 3 kids to show for it. I got married in 2005; had a miscarriage a few months later; had a son a year later; then got pregnant again in mid-2007. I was so excited because echography showed it was a girl. I already had two sons. Which woman wouldn't want to have a princess daughter?

Her pregnancy wasn't like the others as it came with quite a bunch of health complications that surprised me. I had to be on some meds and go for more check-ups than was the case for prior pregnancies. But, like I said, I was excited and couldn't wait to cradle my own Angel.

I even saved to afford a chic private room at the General Hospital in my city, which is considered the reference for the sub-region. You could, therefore imagine my panic when contractions started; it seemed she was in no haste to come. I spent the night in the hospital in pains, being monitored and on drips. She was born the next day, 07.02.19 at noon. Oh, how beautiful she was! She had hair like I did, and you could see it.

I barely cradled my baby when it started, I still can't tell if she was coughing or choking. She was taken away and they put her in an incubator. Her brother David had spent 2 weeks in one too.

'For Heaven's sake, what's happening,' I cried?

But that was the most I could do. Never could I have imagined she would be gone by 4 a.m. the following day; that she would be lifeless the next time we would carry her.

Yes, I remember going to check on her at 4 a.m. and seeing them wrapping her up in a white bed sheet. I could tell as I walked in there in a daze. Her dad had been called by the nurse some 30 minutes earlier and I was too tired to follow. I just walked in there like a madwoman, showed my hands, carried my baby, opened the sheets, gave her a kiss and told her I would try to go on.

I crawled under my hospital bed that day and stayed there for an hour or so, just shaking and groaning. Nobody could get me to come out until I got tired.

Real healing started 3 years later when I left my marriage and country. Depression came alongside a suicide attempt before I left. But I started talking about the pain in 2013. Closure started in 2018 when I did a live video with AC Mbeng of Every Little Life Matters. Ange-Claire would have been 11 this year, but it is well. I got me a flesh of my flesh and blood of my blood guardian angel.

MARIE A. ABANGA.

Douala, Cameroon

A Little Prelude

It all started with the story that pregnancy for me was an impossibility because 1 had a fibroid.

Next was an appointment was booked for a scan for the fibroid to be checked.

Scan done and a date given to for surgery to remove the fibroid.

Within that time, surprisingly, 1 was already pregnant without knowing since 1 was already convinced by what the health professionals told me.

A week before the operation to remove the fibroid, I was booked for a pre-assessment to make sure I was physically, medically and even mentally fit for the procedure.

Before going for that appointment, I had missed my period for 7weeks. However, 1 couldn't tell my husband to avoid giving any false hopes. Unfortunately or fortunately, 1 went alone for this appointment.

I timidly went in when it was my turn. The consultant was welcoming, which helped in calming down my worried nerves.

We talked over things, and one of the questions was, "when was your last period?"

Shaking with tears running down my cheek, I told him when I last had my period. He asked for a urine sample and sent it off to be tested immediately.

Within 5 minutes, the result came back. He looked at it, looked at me 3 good times, got up, gave me a hug and a tissue saying, "Mrs Anguo, cry no more, you are pregnant." I was speechless with complete shock.

I left for home but could not bring myself to break the news to my elder sister, my daughter or my husband. When I finally told my husband two months later, he thought I was joking.

It was only after the first scan that we finally opened up to the rest of the family.

It was a smooth pregnancy until 3 days to the 28th week on New Year's Eve 2004 New Year's around 1am, I felt feverish but got up about 8am and started preparing New Year's dinner. Within an hour I experienced some dizzy spells and thought no one had noticed, but our daughter had already noticed that something was wrong. She came and leaned over with her ear on my tummy to feel the baby's heartbeat as she was used to doing at least 5-6 times a day. Fast forward, my husband rushed me to the hospital in the heart of winter.

The paediatrician who checked me over started fanning me with cold air. I was shivering from 11am until about 3pm crying out with stomach pain, and none of the nurses listened or checked on me again. My husband kept asking when somebody would see me. We were told it was New Year's Day and no Doctors on call. I was moved into a quiet room. The pain was becoming more and more unbearable, and one of the nurses had to give me codeine.

Within 2 hours, I was in labour. By the time my husband supported me into the toilet, there was already blood everywhere.

My husband called out for the nurse, and four paediatricians appeared, our beautiful baby came out, took first and last breath almost at the same time.

Our baby was dressed and brought to us and was placed on my stomach. As a result of the crippling emotions that came with the devastating loss of a loved one, my husband was instantly struck by grief, and as such, he couldn't even carry his own baby. Our first daughter, my sister and her husband were all heartbroken.

- Some well-wishers and nurses wanted us to sue the hospital. My husband said, "What would suing do? We are without our child?"

- My doctor visited and asked if my husband was abusive. I was lost for words. My husband has never forgotten that doctor.

Lessons learnt:

- Nobody can understand your pain

- My husband was completely ignored in the middle of it all. He finally broke his silence in July 2020, during the bereaved parents' awareness month on one of Claris' talk show interviews, where he opened up and finally found closure.

As for me, whenever someone loses a baby, all the sad memories of my baby come back. **Baby Rose Anguo, born 01.01 2005 and died the same day.**

(Immaculate Anguo, UK)

My Journey Through The Loss of a Child

The pain and grief hugs you daily, as the memory of once feeling the movement of the baby, you got very close too, resurface. It's often difficult to explain the pain and anger you go through during this period, to even the dearest/closest one to you-your partner. As they bond you shared with the little man or woman inside you, could only be understood and imagined by you and you alone. This could sometimes lead to you thinking that your spouse and loved ones don't care, thereby triggering you to make this journey to recovery ALONE. However, the big question is; do we really ever recover from this loss or leave it unattended, unresolved and develop coping strategies to deal with the loss to enable us to move on quickly with life?

My journey of losing a child, soon after her birth, left me with some of the feelings and questions described above. While grieving the loss, I was **bitter**, frustrated and angry that my husband had appeared to have moved on quicker than expected. His little or no show of emotions and quick dismissal of my cries of pain, as time went on, made me question if he really understood the magnitude of what had happened to us. His common phrase was, "Dee, no cry noh. God go give we pikin again," (stop crying, and God will bless us with a child again). Most often in anger and frustration, I questioned if that's all that he could tell me. This gradually started impacting negatively on our relationship; more shouting and quarrelling; less laughter and joy in each other's company, fewer outings, etc. However, I felt all I wanted was for him to give me the platform to express all the roller coaster of emotions that I was going through, expecting him to cry, hug and reassure me and go through this journey with me.

It struck me one fateful day when I bumped into my husband silently weeping away in the bedroom. What surprised me wasn't that I found him weeping, but the fact that he quickly tried to dry off the tears running down in cheeks and pretended to put on a brave, smiling and reassuring face. It suddenly dawned on me that perhaps my husband had been grieving and dealing with the loss of our daughter internally, while trying to stay brave, in order for us to move forward.

This set me into reflecting how male ego, coupled with our traditional cultural and religious perspectives, could impact and determine how we deal with sensitive issues like child loss. Exploring these areas and working through all the hoops, we started gradually talking through our feelings and emotions. This was the beginning of us grieving and healing together as a couple. I have come to agree and accept that the pains, feelings and emotions of any woman who has experienced a miscarriage, stillbirth or loss of a child shortly after birth, can ONLY be explained and understood by those who have been through similar situations. With this in mind, I often spared my husband sometimes for "NOT GETTING IT."

I have come to realise that our culture, traditions and Christian faith, continue to create some level of sensitivity around this topic of child loss and my only worry about this is that, if women who have experienced this, aren't given a safe space to talk about it and work through this with their husbands, family and loved ones, it might lead to other underlying problems like relationship break-up, mental health issues, withdrawal, isolation, etc.

Grace Chebe, UK

God be Praised

Three months after our wedding, I became pregnant. There was so much excitement and expectation. Eight weeks after, all the excitement vanished in our home. One night, about 1a.m., I felt this very serious cramping pain in my tummy and was rushed to the hospital by the ambulance. After the scan, the bad news came: I had had a miscarriage. I was heartbroken but was told by the doctors it was normal and there was no explanation and not to worry. After that, I tried to be brave and go about life as though nothing had happened. It was just an 8-week-old foetus, not a child yet. I was consoled. So, I managed to put it behind me and move on quickly.

About 6 months later, I was pregnant again and this time, was put on bed rest for the first trimester. I went through a very challenging 14 weeks and was given the all-clear by the doctor to return to work and live normally as it was now the second trimester and the danger had passed.

We were again very excited. But 2 weeks after the all-clear that sharp pain came back again, and I was back in the hospital. This time, the news almost killed me: the 16-week old full-grown baby, with all parts visible, was dead cold in my womb. The procedure to take out the remains was dreadful, and I almost bled to death.

After that, I felt like a part of me was dead. Take heart, everybody said. But it hurt in the deepest parts of my soul. It felt like my world was crashing. How was I going to get over this one?

One day at a time, I just existed. Then I started hospital follow up session as the doctors wanted to try and identify the reason for the late miscarriage. These hospital sessions meant I met other women who had had similar experiences. Interacting with these women and sharing our experiences seemed to work magic for me. I gradually healed as I talked and listened more to others with similar challenges.

For women, it's been made to look like talking about the processes of losing a pregnancy is some sort of taboo. We bury the pain within, and nobody ever gets to understand what we really feel. If we are not careful, we slump into depression as a consequence and nobody really understands. For me, talking about it and interacting with other women who had gone through the same thing made a huge difference. We should encourage more women to talk out and release that pain within. It sure helps. Now I have two beautiful girls. God be praised!

Judith Moor

London, England

Talking has Strengthened My Marriage

Two months before my marriage introduction, I found out I was pregnant. We were so excited at the prospect of the double blessings of marriage and a baby. When I was 4 months gone, I started having stomach aches. I lost the pregnancy when I was rushed to the hospital. I was so crushed and almost attempted suicide but thanks to help and support from family and doctors, I was comforted and made to understand that everything was going to be alright.

6 months later, after my bride price was paid, I found out I was expectant again. 2 months into my pregnancy, I started spotting and doctors put me on mandatory bed rest, assuring me everything was under control. One fateful morning, that was 7 April 2019, I woke up in a pool of blood. When I got to the hospital, I was told it was an incomplete miscarriage. I had a number of appointments with doctors and finally underwent dilation and curettage (D&C).

After this, I got so bitter with myself, my husband and even lost friends. I would lock myself in the house and cry myself out. But a friend who had been through a similar experience referred me to a Facebook page (Every Little Life Matters – The Davi-Jayce Foundation). Through that, I talked to Claris–founder of the aforementioned foundation– who advised I talk about how I felt and what I was going through and also write to my unborn. This has been very helpful in my healing process. Also, I get to visit the maternity ward when I feel empty. I'm slowly healing and remain hopeful I will have a child soon. I'm happy talking about this. Talking has strengthened my marriage as I used to be more focused on the loss and had neglected my Man.

Nelly Mart - Nairobi

Chapter Six
Poems of Grief

I may by no means come anywhere close to being a great poet, but my grief inked my quill and my tears dissipated my fears. Courage was mine to write what I felt without bothering how it read. A broken soul was I; broken poems I wrote. The need for an ocean in which to plunge beckoned and my ink readily and generously stretched in front of my weeping and burning soul for a quench.

Don't be alarmed should my poor lines leave your cerebrum with a sour sensation like that of a sour fruit on the tooth as you voyage from one line to another in your soberness. Carelessly dotted here and there, the stains are like trees in the wild. Pick what you can and let the forest stay. It's heart over arts to paint this pain. May the sweet memories of him indelibly stain my soul till we meet again never to part!

#1And they said, "Sorry"

She went for a pee
There was a leak

But she thought it was just a wee

She went back to sleep in a swift
Then, she felt adrift
Yet, she thought it was just a shift
She carried on as normal
Though in deep thoughts
Wondering what's about to happen
Then Dr Google played the trick
The clock started to tick

While she drove to work
She pondered about the what ifs
Her mind was in a wonder
She was in a ponder
If history was going to repeat itself
Yet, she drove
Because life has to continue
No matter what
She went for a pee again

There she was in disbelief
'Brown Hot chocolate found'!!
Which is not supposed to happen
Not during this period, anyway
As if it was all ok
SHE walked out, over and round the building
Making sure no one was alarmed.

Upon examination
They looked at each other
Without uttering a word
But she knew the meaning of that look
She knew what they were going to say

When she walked over
All she said was
"Sorry".
With eyes closed,
Breath held, memory lane revisited
12 years back, same words
"Sorry"
Explanations given
Decisions made
Another pee she went

1,2,3 steps

There, right there in the middle of the room

It all happened

Heaven broke loose

She swiftly turned around in panic

She thought someone just poured a bucket of water down
her

Behold!

In amazement and shock

Her precious, jealously protected bucket of water had just
leaked down her legs

She cried, she wept

On her knees, she begged Him above to reverse the situation

As you see, it was way too late

The deed was already done

Her life was never going to be the same again

Initially, she thought she couldn't live after this

But, look, she lives

She smiles though through tears

With a broken heart

However, not broken

Why?

Because **"She's got Grit"**.

(C.Angafor)

You don't know what pain is...

You don't know what pain is until
All you've got is pain
You don't know what pain is until
You've been restlessly pacing the room
Letting your troubled steps echo from the stairs
Forcing your mind to drag your numb body
Pining away in the desolate corridors
Trying a clumsy dance on a special labour ball
And not really knowing what next

You don't know what pain is until
You do a scan and there is no foetus
And then you remember: oh! The bleed
But don't understand why baby had to leap

You don't know what labour pain is until
You've pushed out a beautiful bundle of joy, yet, lifeless
And cradle its eternally-slumbering body in your arms
Still feeling like you're simply just caught in a nightmare

You don't know what pain is until
You've laboured for hours and had to push
Push out a piece of joy whose cry you'll never hear

Who'll never say, I love you or I hate you, mum
A baby whose name you'll never call and get a response
Or whose footsteps the staircase will never know

You don't know what pain is until
You've plodded down that aisle
And in your arms is a dismal white casket
Instead of a beautiful white bouquet

You don't know what pain is until
Everyone thinks you're crazy with grief
Because they've never been there before
And tag your baby "unborn" or "just a miscarriage"

You don't know what pain is until
The cemetery knows your footsteps and wardrobe
Because you believe that's your second home
And you don't want to feel like you've abandoned your
Angel.

You know what pain is
When all you've got is that pain.

(C.Angafor)

1 hour 20 mins

The 80 minutes we shared felt like a lifetime of love,

A lifetime of knowing him,

A lifetime of cuddling,

Bonding and friendship.

It equally feels like a lifetime of missing him,

My love, and a lifetime of having our heartbeats synchronised.

Special love to all Angels gone too soon,

Be it through miscarriage or stillbirth.

Or those who fought to be born alive or

Live but couldn't be given the chance because they were
deemed just a little too early.

Farewell my little Cherished Beloved Healer Angel.

You fulfilled your purpose here on earth and

Returned to your Father Just like Jesus did.

Your little life on earth filled our hearts with lots of love.

The love you brought and left numbed the pain of the ordeal.

1 hour 20 minutes you lived

1 hour 20 minutes you left a lasting vacuum

1 hour 20 minutes that redefined my life

In 1 hour 20 minutes, you painted the bigger picture

You solved the puzzle that puzzles the universe

Life and death are great cousins

Tomorrow is just an illusion.

(C N..Angafor)

2017: Dark to Dawn

A year of happiness

A year of sadness

A year of joy and sorrow

A year where I made new friends and lost some old ones

A year where I turned a big milestone in my life

A year of forty

The year where I reunited with my father's family

Happiest and most sorrowful year of my life

A year of lofty dreams and high expectations

A year of death and rebirth

D-J's departure marked a new me

A new page was flipped.

(C.N. Angafor)

Angel

Angel of mine

Too soon born

Too soon gone

Perish never

Cherished ever

Beloved Healer

God-given shield

The deal you sealed

And returned to Him

Like your name you still remain

Our Cherished Beloved Healer

You're proof that God shields.

(Gicles Angafor)

God Had Better Plans

Two weeks before September 11
Your first suit I had just bought.
On it shone "2 My cutest little brother."
Two weeks before September 11
Mum broke the news to me.
Then I remembered, Ah!
That was her imaginary friend
She'd been telling me about.
Then I recalled Lesra and I had to be careful
When playing around Mummy's Tummy.
Then I understood why the tons of hospital appointments.
The thought of a little brother was all-consuming.
All I wished for was a little brother
Who'd call me big brother
Kid bro was a dream-come-true for me.
But mum and I made a pinky swear
To keep it on the hush-hush.
Till mummy said so, I had to fight the urge.
We had plans with him and for him:
Plans to play our own games together;
Plans to teach him how to build Lego;
Plans to teach him how to communicate with Lesra;
Plans for Lesra to show him how to use his Ipad;

Plans to always take care of him since he was our little brother;

Plans to protect him from danger;

To jump on the trampoline;

Read books together.

Now that God decided to make you an Angel in Heaven

I won't cry; I won't weep,

Though every hair on my head wants me to.

I asked mom lots of questions:

Lesra was born premature and survived

Why did Davi-Jayce have to die?

Was mummy ill because baby kicked her tummy?

Lesra was premature and now is autistic.

Did autism take my little brother's life away?

Davi-Jayce, when I saw you in your little cot,

I thought you were so tiny.

I wished for you to open your eyes and look at me,

But it never happened.

Even though you will never have to grow with us,

I will always love you.

I want to thank you for making me a big brother

Thank you for making my mummy a, happier

And even stronger woman, though in your absence.

Thank you for shielding and healing my family.

I will always love you

Too soon you came.

Too soon you left.

In our hearts forever

Your memories live on

Love!

(Gicles/Lesra)

Judge Me Not

Judge me not:
Based on my circumstances
Based on my situation
Based on my problems
Based on how I feel
Or on how I react
Do not decide for me
Let me be my decision maker
Let me be the one to decide on how I feel
How I react
Let me decide on what makes me happy
What makes me angry
Do not hold back any information or message from me
Because you do not know how I will react
No matter how bad it may be, tell me
Let me be the one to choose
Let me be the one to decide
Let me know
Let me be involved
Do not pity or ignore me
Or make me isolate myself based on my experiences
Because you do not know how I feel
Let me be my judge
Because in the end
It would have been my life
My happiness
My health
And I would have decided on what to do with me.
(C.N. Angafor)

PLEASE DON'T

Please do not tell me God did not want me to suffer anymore
Forgetting to know that the same God lets people suffer for a reason
And that that there is suffering for love
Please do not tell me you now like "the me" you see.
Do not tell me I have become so happy, bold and courageous
When all you could see before was a shy miserable me
I was hoping you'd look past my pain that couldn't be explained
How could you have failed to look beyond my circumstances?
People are neither their problems nor their misery
Sadness or misfortunes or sufferings are only temporal
Every beautiful smile veils a story, usually tragic
But it takes time for the frown to crease into a smile
So please do not judge me based on what you see on the outside
Do not tell me God does not give you what you cannot handle
Rather tell me that God will help me handle what I have been given.

(C.N. Angafor)

Decide Not for Me

Based on my circumstances
Based on my situation
Based on my problems
Based on how I feel
Or on how I react
Do not decide for me
Let me be my decision maker
Let me be the one to decide on how I feel
How I react
Let me decide on what makes me happy
What makes me angry
Do not hold back any information or message from me
Because you do not know how I will react
Let me be aware no matter how bad it is
Let me be the one to choose
Let me be the one to decide
Let me know
Let me be involved
Do not pity me or ignore me
Or make me isolate myself based on my experiences
Because you do not know how I feel
Let me be my judge
Because in the end
It would have been my life
My happiness
My health
And I would have decided on what to do with me.
(C.N.Angafor)

Claris aka AC's
Grief to Grit Summarised

In November 2004, she moved to the UK to join her husband.

March 2005, she lost her baby at just 8 weeks gestation. Then, she didn't know exactly what grief was, but deep within her, she was not ok. However, she carried on as usual with the hidden pain. New in a foreign country, she had no friends yet, there was no mum or sister to comfort her but her husband. Some months along the line, she smiled again with a bundle of joy peacefully and healthily growing within her. She was at peace with herself, and she jealously protected her little bundle of joy as the months rolled by. As if the tragedies had not yet started, her baby arrived extremely premature at 24 weeks gestation. At first, she never believed he would live, but she was told her son was ok although he was going to be taken to the Neonatal Intensive Care Unit. At that point, she forgot all about her hidden pain and dedicated her time, her life in making sure her son was going to be ok. That little son has grown into a happy, fine, gorgeous, caring and adorable young man. Even though he is growing up differently-abled, the love and care she has for him surpasses every challenge she has ever been through. Often times, she questions God why He had to allow go through all these, not knowing that the "Why" was still going to be revealed. As the years went by, God was still at work with her. She had another little boy, unfortunately, this time, she was hit by postnatal depression. However, she refused to be medicated because she believed she could handle it. Life till this stage had been a whole book filled with pages of information, but she was the only one to read and understand what was already written in that book.

Sometimes in life, tragedies and pain blind us from seeing the bigger picture or from reading and understanding what has already been written in the book. She still pulled along, always with a cloud of sadness lingering above her face, that most often showed itself in the form of mood swings, crying and sometimes anger. Friends and family saw it as anger issues, but she knew she was struggling and was crying out for help, but no one understood. However, her sons kept her going, and somehow she maintained her smile, though, it wasn't as broad as it is now.

Years down the line, at the age of 40 and just when she was discovering herself and trying to understand the bigger picture in all that had been happening in her life, God in his infinite mercy and love decided to bless her with another bundle of joy. This time around, she was excited but confused and at the same time, questioned God's decision. However, God works in mysterious ways, and at times he answers past prayers. We all know that God does not necessarily answer our prayers when the request is made.

As soon as she accepted, acknowledged and embraced her new reality of being a preggy at 40, another tragedy hit. Her little baby boy was born prematurely again. This time around, he lived for 1h20mins. She said welcome and goodbye almost at the same time.

To her saddest amazement, this was the peak of the grief she had been going through over the years unknowingly. This hit her so badly because apparently, she had not properly grieved the previous incidents in her life. She had been suffering with ungrieved or suppressed grief. However, she was determined to get back on her feet.

Although very painful, she gave herself time to understand why all this had been happening to her for years. She carefully went through all the stages of grief. This gave her a better understanding of the emotions she had been experiencing without knowing why. It was therefore revealed during this period that she had been grieving for years without knowing, which somehow, concluded that she has had depression for years. You can count the years from above right?

It got to the point where her doctor would call, check on her and encourage her to agree to be medicated. Doctors do not randomly call a patient without an appointment, but hers did almost 3 times in a week. She finally accepted.

This was the point in her life that the bigger picture; the purpose of every experience lived was beginning to reveal itself. She had almost given up everything and everyone at some point. However, she constantly had to remind herself of how far she has come.

You see, she has gone through some real-life challenging and complex issues in her life, but she has never given up. Tenacity, strength, love, hope and grit and a robust support system have been her tools. As she looks back into all she has been through, she understands that one should never underestimate their experiences. Every experience is a teacher, a future builder; every experience, no matter how sad, is a lesson to be learned and a new you to be born.

Today, she actively participates in events both in the UK and abroad. These events take place in various community centres, conferences and workshops, all focused on autism/disability, mental health and/or other social issues plaguing the communities.

On International Women's day 2020, she was honoured with two awards. Mother of the Year award, in recognition and in celebration of the marvellous work she does with families and the positive difference she makes in the lives of parents and their children. She was also named as one of the 100 most inspirational women in the world. As if the awards were not yet enough in a year, in October 2020, during the Black History month celebrations, she was awarded as a Community Achiever in Basingstoke.

She is a Special Needs Parent Coach, a mentor, a mental health advocate and a Pregnancy and Infant loss Advocate, all based on her lived experience.

She is an autism Ambassador, an advocate, an inspirational speaker, a Data Validator at the NHS, she is the Founder and Owner of CAN-Abilities and Every Little Life matters Foundations. She is now a proud author of the book you're reading right now; GRIEF TO GRIT: A touching tale of Love, Loss, Pain and Tenacity. This piece documents how she conquered grief and gained grit".

Through experiences, over the years, she's discovered that most individuals who have gone through similar experiences have not yet given a voice to their challenges, which in a way, hinders their healing process.

She, therefore, set up an online streaming talk show, "The Voice of Hope Media". This is a safe space created to give a voice to those societal issues which many individuals see as taboo, too sensitive, or too emotional. Here, individuals are encouraged to share their experiences which may lead to healing or to others being inspired. Sharing may lead to someone being able to help them or point them in the right direction. She uses this platform as a vehicle to educate, empower, inspire and give hope to everyone affected by these complex life issues, so they will be able to realise that every experience lived, is valuable, worthy and has the power to transform lives.

"The Voice of Hope Media," is made up of a group of specialists/professionals ranging from parents, medical professionals, teachers, mental health advocates, special needs parent coaches and barristers who use evidence-based experiences to support, mentor, coach and refer individuals for appropriate help where and when needed.

Today, she believes that "Every experience lived, is valuable, worthy and has the power to transform lives.

NOW, she is the LEADING VOICE OF HOPE AND EMPOWERMENT.

AND SHE IS CLARIS N.ANGAFOR

Are you burdened right now? Turn it into a blessing.

Going through a mess in your life right now? Write a beautiful message from that mess.

Struggling with grief? let it become your GRIT

Going through some form of pain, why not turn it into gain?

Turn your crises into classes and educate, empower, inspire and give hope to others. There are many out there who just need to hear your story and be healed.

Why not give it a voice?

References:

Kubler – Russ, E, (1969) on Death and Dying

https://www.healthline.com/health/pregnancy/rainbow-baby#The-symbolism-of-a-rainbow

https://positivepsychology.com/what-is-resilience/

Resources

These are some of the books and sites that I found incredibly helpful. They may be able to help someone else out there.

Sands (Stillbirth & neonatal death charity) - https://www.sands.org.uk/

SAYING GOODBYE - Zoe Clark-Coates https://www.sayinggoodbye.org/

Ask Me His Name: Learning to live and laugh again after the loss of my baby (**Elle Wright**)

Baby Bliss Charity - https://www.bliss.org.uk/

About the Author

When you think of a lady who is an embodiment of strength, confidence and hope, you are thinking of the inspirational and trailblazing 43-year-old British Cameroonian born, Claris N.Angafor aka (AC Mbeng). She is the most resilient woman you'll find and who wears a smile of hope no matter what time you meet her. Claris is a Special Needs Parent Coach and Mentor in mental health, a Pregnancy and Infant loss Advocate, with lived experiences as an autism Ambassador, Author, inspirational speaker, a Data Validator at the NHS, and Founder and Owner of CAN-Abilities Foundation, and Every Little Life matters Foundation - where she runs an online streaming talk show "The Voice of Hope Media".

Claris holds a BSc in Management from the University of Buea, Cameroon, an MSc in Information Systems Management from the University of London South Bank and a Postgraduate in Autism and Asperger from Sheffield Hallam University.

She moved to the UK in 2004, where she lives with her husband and their five children; a beautiful daughter, two adorable boys here on Earth, one of whom is autistic and the other two in heaven. She has recently been blessed with the gift of a gorgeous grandson. Claris has over the years dedicated her life to looking after her 14-year-old autistic son.

Claris is a leading voice of hope and empowerment. Through her Platforms; CAN-Abilities Foundation, Every Little Life matters Foundation and her an online streaming talk show; "the Voice of Hope Media," she has done a lot of amazing work within communities both in the UK and abroad. All her work is geared towards providing support and giving hope to families and individuals facing complex, life-challenging issues and with Special educational Needs through education, empowerment and inspiration.

Claris also actively participates in events in various community centres, conferences and workshops both in the UK and abroad all focused on autism/disability, mental health and/or other social issues plaguing our communities. On International Women's day this year, Claris was honoured with two awards; Mother of the Year award, in recognition and celebration of the marvellous works she does with families and the positive difference she makes in their lives. She was also named as one of the 100 most inspirational women in the world.

Claris believes that every experience lived, is valuable, worthy and has the power to transform lives. So by sharing her experiences, especially on autism, Claris educates, empowers, gives hope and encourages parents/caregivers to be able to provide the best care and support to autistic individuals, promote their wellbeing in order for them to meet their full potentials. She believes that by breaking the silence that still surrounds autism, disability, pregnancy, infant loss and mental health, the world will become a better place to live in; a place where everyone will be able to speak up, speak out and know that they are worthy, included and valued.

Claris' love and care for her autisic son enabled her to gain a wealth of experience and knowledge. This has allowed her to be a coach and mentor to families through guiding, directing and giving tips on how parents of autistic children can help their children in areas of challenging behaviours, delayed speech, toileting, general advice on what to do when they suspect their child is autistic and most importantly on how a parent can take care of themselves in order to avoid the effects of Special needs Burn out.

Many special needs and bereaved parents do struggle to come to terms with their new reality and so struggle at some point with their mental health. Claris' structured one-on-one talks with them enable them to go through the stages of grief to be able to live a fulfilled life.

Claris is a passionate, resilient, dedicated and caring individual who sees the good in every person irrespective of their abilities. She believes that every child deserves to be well looked after, loved, understood, accepted and given a chance to flourish in their full potentials. In her word, "disability is just a mindset, we're all part of one big family and must live as such, showing love and giving support because that's the right thing to do." Stretch a hand and pull a soul from the abyss of despondency today. We're trapped in this world together; no life is superior to another, every little life matters'.

Check out more of Claris's work on

https://www.canabilities.org/

https://www.youtube.com/c/TheNsangliShowWithACMbeng

https://www.facebook.com/thevoiceofhopemediaTVHM/

MARCIA M
PUBLISHING HOUSE

www.marciampublishing.com